BRIGHT NOTES

THE GLASS MENAGERIE AND A STREETCAR NAMED DESIRE BY TENNESSEE WILLIAMS

Intelligent Education

INFLUENCE PUBLISHERS

Nashville, Tennessee

BRIGHT NOTES: The Glass Menagerie and A Streetcar Named Desire
www.BrightNotes.com

ISBN: 978-1-645424-16-1 (Paperback)
ISBN: 978-1-645424-17-8 (eBook)

Published in accordance with the U.S. Copyright Office Orphan Works and Mass Digitization report of the register of copyrights, June 2015.

Originally published by Monarch Press.
James Lamar Roberts; Gilbert L. Rathbun, 1965
2020 Edition published by Influence Publishers.

Interior design by Lapiz Digital Services. Cover Design by Thinkpen Designs.

Printed in the United States of America.

Library of Congress Cataloging-in-Publication Data forthcoming.
Names: Intelligent Education
Title: BRIGHT NOTES: The Glass Menagerie and A Streetcar Named Desire
Subject: STU004000 STUDY AIDS / Book Notes

CONTENTS

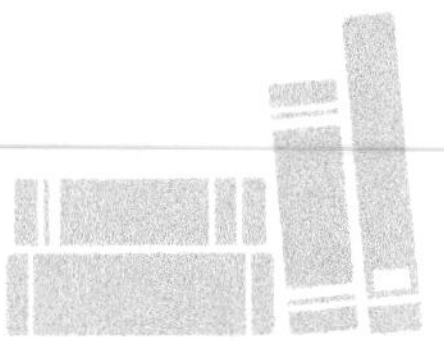

TENNESSEE WILLIAMS

IMPORTANT DATES IN THE LIFE OF TENNESSEE WILLIAMS

The data in this section were collected from many newspapers, magazines, and periodicals. This information is important, as it attest to the popular success of Tennessee Williams.

1911

March 26-Thomas Lanier Williams born in Columbus, Mississippi, where maternal grandfather was a minister in the Episcopal Church; childhood illnesses gave extra time for reading many books.

1918

Family moved to St. Louis when Williams was about eight years old. This move to the ugliness of urban life had a harsh effect on him and his slightly infirm sister; led to the beginning of certain neuroses in Williams.

1930

Published first story in *Weird Tales*.

1931 TO 1934

Attended University of Missouri for three years; joined a fraternity, flunked R.O.T.C., won small prizes in poetry and prose, and discovered that alcohol was a sure cure for shyness.

1934 TO 1936

Went to work in a shoe company due to the Depression. Nervous breakdown, attributed to long days in warehouse and to nights of writing. Spent year of recuperation with grandfather who had retired and moved to Memphis.

1936

Attended Washington University, St. Louis; won first prize sponsored by the Webster Groves Little Theater for a one-act play; Williard Howard, director of the Mummers, asked for a play on anti-militarism, *Cairo! Shanghai! Bombay!*, produced in Memphis.

1937

Withdrew from Washington University.

1938 TO 1940

Received B.A. degree from University of Iowa; wrote *Spring Storm* for seminar in playwriting; rewrote *Fugitive Kind* into *Not About Nightingales*; went to New Orleans where he was a waiter in the French Quarter; won $100 for one-act plays; returned to St. Louis; finished *Battle of Angels*.

1940 TO 1942

Received Rockefeller Grant of $1000 with the assistance of Audrey Wood; rewrote *Battle of Angels*, produced in Boston by the Theater Guild, bad reviews, closed; heart condition led to 4F classification by the draft board; first operation on left eye for cataract; small Rockefeller Grant; lived in New Orleans; second operation on left eye; worked as elevator operator and usher in New York.

1942

Audrey Wood secures $250-a-week contract at M.G.M., two scripts rejected; worked on *The Glass Menagerie* script, refused by M.G.M.

1943

National Institute of Arts and Letters Citation.

1944

Award from American Academy of Arts and Letters and $1000; *The Glass Menagerie* opened in Chicago on December 26 to rave reviews.

1945

New York opening of *The Glass Menagerie* (561 performances, closing August 3, 1946); April 10, won New York Critics' Circle Award for 1944-1945 on the first ballot. After another eye operation, wrote *The Poker Night*, later incorporated in *A Streetcar Named Desire*; *You Touched Me* opened September 25 in New York for 100 performances.

1946 TO 1947

Twenty-seven Wagons Full of Cotton; *Stairs to the Roof*, written in 1941, produced at Pasadena Community Playhouse, **theme** used later in *Camino Real*; Actors Laboratory Theater in Southern California produced *Mooney's Kid Don't Cry, Portrait of a Madonna*, and *The Last of My Solid Gold Watches*.

1947

A Streetcar Named Desire opened in New York on December 3 for 855 performances, closed December 17, 1949; won Pulitzer Prize for 1947-1948; won a second New York Critics' Circle Award for 1947-1948; *You Touched Me* published by Samuel French.

1948

Summer and Smoke opened in New York City October 6 for 100 performances, closed on January 1, 1949; first visit to Rome and Paris.

1950

Roman Spring of Mrs. Stone published by New Directions.

1951

The Rose Tattoo opened February 3 in New York City for 306 performances, closed October 27, 1951.

1952

Won election to National Institute of Arts and Letters. *Summer and Smoke* revived off-Broadway; directed by Jose Quintero, and starring Geraldine Page.

1953

Camino Real opened March 19 in New York City for 60 performances, closed May 9, 1953.

1955

Cat on a Hot Tin Roof opened on March 24 in New York City and closed November 17, 1956; won Pulitzer Prize for 1954-1955 (Williams' second); won Critic's Circle Award for 1954-1955 (Williams' third); *Twenty-Seven Wagons Full of Cotton* produced as part of All in One in New York.

1956

Baby Doll, the film, opened in New York City December 18; *The Glass Menagerie, A Streetcar Named Desire, Summer and Smoke, Camino Real* staged in London.

1957

Orpheus Descending opened in New York City, March 21 for 68 performances.

1958

Garden District (Something Unspoken and Suddenly Last Summer) opened off-Broadway January 7 at playwright's request; *Mooney's Kid Don't Cry, The Last of the Solid Gold Watches, This Property Is Condemned* produced on television by Kraft Theater.

1959

Sweet Bird of Youth opened in New York City March 10 for 95 performances; *Portrait of a Madonna* produced as part of Triple

Play April 15; first trip to Far East. *The Purification*, single Anta production.

1960

Period of Adjustment opened in New York City November 10, closed March 4, 1961.

1961

Night of the Iguana opened late in December in New York City, best dramatic form since *Streetcar*.

1962

The Milk Train Doesn't Stop Here Anymore opened in New York City, complete failure. Williams totally revised the play.

1963

The Milk Train Doesn't Stop Here Anymore. Directed by Tony Richardson.

1964

Night of the Iguana made into film.

1965

The Glass Menagerie opened in New York City on May 4 to commemorate the 20th anniversary of its original opening in 1945.

TENNESSEE WILLIAMS

INTRODUCTION

He was born on March 26, 1911, in the Episcopal rectory of his grandfather in Columbus, Mississippi. Christened Thomas Lanier, he was the second child and first son of Cornelius Coffin Williams, a traveling salesman for a shoe company, and Edwina Dakin Williams, the daughter of the local rector.

When young Williams was eight years old, his father was promoted to a managerial position with his company's subsidiary in St. Louis. Leaving the rural, leisurely life in Mississippi, the family moved to St. Louis. For Williams, and for his older sister Rose, the uprooting was violent. Throughout his adolescence and youth the family lived in a succession of small apartments which were a far cry from the comfortable home of his childhood. A sensitive youth, his life became increasingly interior. He was extremely close to his mother and sister, but felt little affection for his father, whose bluntness and rough manner alienated the boy.

EARLY INTEREST IN WRITING

When Williams was eleven years old, his mother bought him a typewriter, and from that moment he began to turn out works of fact and fiction by the carload. Once he began writing he did not stop for a day. Poems, vignettes, sketches and short stories flickered to life. His abundant imagination had found the perfect means for expression. After graduating from high school, he entered the University of Missouri, where he spent two years as a journalism major. By now it was 1932, the height of the Depression, and Williams' academic career came to a halt when his father withdrew him from college and shuttled him into a position as clerk with his firm. Williams' three years with the shoe company were probably the most difficult and unhappy of his entire life. The drudgery was endless and his anguish was intensified by his inability to find time to pursue his writing. Unable to write during the day, he tried to write in the evenings and into the night. Finally the inevitable happened: the combination of long hours of work he hated and long nights of subsistence on coffee and cigarettes took its toll. He suffered a breakdown. Fortunately, he recovered rapidly and was sent to his grandparents' home, now in Tennessee, to convalesce. That summer, Williams wrote his first play, a comedy called *Cairo! Shanghai! Bombay!*, about two sailors on shore leave who become involved in a series of riotous adventures. It was presented at a small summer theatre and its warm reception encouraged the young writer to continue with playwriting.

Free of the shoe company, he enrolled at Washington University, St. Louis, where he hoped to complete his education. His imagination fired by writers like Anton Chekhov and D. H. Lawrence, he turned out a second play, *The Magic Tower*, which was produced in 1936 by a local theatre group. He entered the senior class at Washington University and joined a dynamic group of young actors and writers called The Mummers. Stimulated by his association with this exciting and invigorating troupe, Williams wrote two more dramas, a one-act pacifist play called *Headlines*, and a full-length drama entitled *Me, Vashya!*, which dealt with a munitions maker who during World War I sold his products alternately to the highest bidders.

FAMILY TROUBLES

Despite his newly discovered vocation, Williams' final year at Washington University was a dismal one. His general apathy for the classroom was one reason. Another was his issue with the school over a matter of policy. But something much more serious than school setbacks was preying on his mind during the years of 1936 and 1937. The relationship between his parents was becoming increasingly hostile. In a few years it would disintegrate into a separation; now it made home life difficult. In the midst of this friction and despair another **catastrophe** was evolving. Rose Williams was succumbing to mental illness. The anguish Williams felt at this was almost unbearable. She had been almost his exclusive companion during childhood and the ties between them were intensely close. Nine years later, after Rose was hopelessly committed to an institution, Williams would pay his most moving tribute to her in his semi-autobiographical drama, *The Glass Menagerie*. But in 1936, in the midst of extreme despair, Williams turned to his writing with an almost demoniac intensity. *Candles to the Sun*, a violent story of the exploitation of Alabama coal miners, was too strong for the stomachs of many critics when it was produced by the Mummers, although it received a generally enthusiastic response from audiences in St. Louis.

INITIAL SUCCESS AND FAILURE

In 1937 Rose was sent to an institution and Williams' final tie with his home and family was broken. He had been dropped from Washington University more from a lack of interest than anything else, but as autumn came around he again became determined to complete college. Feeling he needed a change of atmosphere, he enrolled at the University of Iowa, where he wrote three plays. The first, *The Fugitive Kind*, was sent act by act to the Mummers in St. Louis who produced it in 1938. It dealt with the dredges of humanity and was replete with stock characters including the beautiful but "lost" heroine. Williams' other two plays at Iowa were written for the late Professor E. C. Mabie's seminar in playwriting. *Spring Storm* was a play very specifically about love. *Not About Nightingales*, begun at Iowa and completed in St. Louis during the summer of 1938, was about a prison riot based upon an actual occurrence at the time. The Mummers were eager to produce it but the Depression had finally taken its toll. In financial straits, they were unable to go on and they disbanded before they could stage the play.

In the spring of 1938, Williams received his Bachelor's degree from the University of Iowa. He returned to St. Louis for a few months, then journeyed to New Orleans where he hoped to join the W.P.A. Writers' Project. He was unsuccessful but he remained in New Orleans during the autumn and winter of 1938. He felt thoroughly at ease in the Bohemian atmosphere of the old city, and he marked what he felt to be his newly found liberation with a change of name. He dropped the name Thomas and dubbed himself Tennessee. That winter he wrote one-act plays dealing for the most part with the individual's struggle for freedom in the face of hopeless odds. Almost all these short plays manifested an acute social consciousness on the part of their author.

The turning point in Williams' life presented itself quite unobtrusively. Through a small article in a paper he learned that the Group Theatre in New York was sponsoring a playwriting contest. He submitted his four long plays, *Candles to the Sun*, *The Fugitive Kind*, *Spring Storm*, and *Not About Nightingales*, together with a group of his one-actors which he named *American Blues*. Not only did Williams win an award from the Group Theatre for the *American Blues* selection, but, more importantly for him, he won the admiration of theatrical agent Audrey Wood, whose friend Molly Day Thatcher was one of the Group Theatre's judges. Miss Wood contacted the young writer and he became her client. While he continued to write she began to see what financial assistance she could get for him. She succeeded admirably, obtaining a Rockefeller grant enabling Williams to come to New York. In New York he enrolled at the New School for Social Research, where John Gassner and Theresa Helburn were conducting a playwriting seminar. It was here that Williams completed a play which he had begun earlier, *Battle of Angels*. With Gassner's help, the Theatre Guild took an option on it and prepared to open it in New York in the winter of 1941. But after an unsuccessful pre-Broadway engagement the drama closed in Boston and Williams' first big opportunity ended in failure. He was to wait five years for another chance. In the meantime he continued to write. He turned out short stories and poems, some of which were published in small literary magazines; he revised *Battle of Angels*; and he worked on new plays. He completed a one-act drama about the last days of D. H. Lawrence, which he titled *I Rise In Flame, Cried the Phoenix*. Early in 1942 he completed a full-length play called *Stairs to the Roof*, which is a fantasy about a young man who liberates himself from the drudgery of a job with a shirt manufacturer very similar to the shoe company in which Williams had worked. He also wrote a play in collaboration with a friend, Donald Windham. It was called *You Touched Me!* and was based upon a short story of the same name by D. H. Lawrence. To support himself while writing, Williams took a variety of odd jobs from a night elevator operator to a waiter in an all-night cafe. He roamed from New York to Florida, living a hand-to-mouth existence as he sought new material and new inspiration. In the spring of 1943, through the efforts of Audrey Wood, Williams obtained a position as a scriptwriter for Metro-Goldwyn-Mayer Studios in Hollywood. But he soon found that he did not care for his new vocation. He listlessly worked on a few scenarios, but spent most of his time on an original screenplay titled *The Gentleman Caller*. He submitted it to the studio but it was rejected, so he refashioned it into a stage play and renamed it *The Glass Menagerie*.

The play was optioned to producer-director-actor Eddie Dowling, who cast the aging Laurette Taylor in the role of the mother and himself as the narrator, Tom Wingfield. At first nothing seemed to go well. There was bickering among the members of the company, Miss Taylor seemed to be unsteady in the part, and as the troupe arrived in Chicago for the pre-Broadway opening in December of 1944, a pall of gloom seemed to hang over everyone. But on opening night, December 26, the pall was dispelled in a burst of theatrical radiance. Miss Taylor gave a luminous performance and the critics were lavish in their praise of her and of the play and its author. Even after this auspicious beginning, hard luck continued to haunt *The Glass Menagerie*. Despite the glowing reviews, the play failed to draw audiences and the producers decided to close it. But again the press came to the rescue. The Chicago drama critics exhorted the public to attend the new drama, and slowly at first, and then in increasing numbers, the public attended. By the end of its third week in Chicago, *The Glass Menagerie* was playing to full and enthusiastic houses. On March 31, 1945, the play opened in New York to immediate critical and popular acclaim, and on April 1, after more than fifteen years of continual effort and disappointment, Tennessee Williams was being hailed as an overnight success.

FURTHER SUCCESS AND THE PULITZER PRIZE

With *The Glass Menagerie* an established hit, Williams and Donald Windham began to prepare their collaboration, *You Touched Me!*, for Broadway. It opened only six months after *The Glass Menagerie*. The latter was still enjoying a successful run, and *'You Touched Me!* paled considerably by the inevitable critical comparison. A slight play, without the depth of characterization found in *The Glass Menagerie, You Touched Me!* managed a modest run of a few months. But Williams was already immersed in work on two new dramas, *Summer and Smoke* and *The Poker Night*. He finished them almost at the same time and retitled *The Poker Night* as *A Streetcar Named Desire*. It opened first, on December 3, 1947, and confirmed the talent and promise inherent in *The Glass Menagerie*. Unanimously hailed by critics and audiences alike, it was subsequently awarded both the Drama Critics' Circle Award and the Pulitzer Prize, and it established its creator as the leading American playwright of his generation. *Summer and Smoke* opened in October of 1948 to a mixed critical reception. Like *You Touched Me!*, it had the misfortune to open when it could still be compared with a Williams success still playing on Broadway. It had a moderate run, and Williams, disappointed, returned to his writing.

He continued to work on *Battle Of Angels*, which, since its failure in Boston, eight years before, had become a kind of private obsession with him. He wrote a few short stories which he collected with some earlier ones into a volume called *One Arm*. In a few years a second collection of stories entitled *Hard Candy* would also be published. Two new works evolved out of a few months' time he spent in Italy. One was a novella called *The Roman Spring of Mrs. Stone* and the other a play, *The Rose Tattoo*. Williams had written the latter with the tempestuous Italian actress, Anna Magnani, in mind, but she was unable to perform in it (although she later played in the movie version). The drama, which opened on February 3,1951, was a moderate success. In 1953 Williams tasted failure in his cruelest professional reversal since the collapse of *Battle of Angels*. His most ambitious undertaking, *Camino Real*, was a flop on Broadway. Since *A Streetcar Named Desire* six years before, his works had been greeted with diminishing enthusiasm by critics and audiences alike. Williams was plagued by doubts. He was not getting younger and to all apparent purposes he had attained his artistic peak six years previously. The following year was a difficult one for the playwright. He continued to write but could not shake the feeling that possibly all his efforts were in vain. He again returned to *Battle of Angels*, determined to justify the drama which he felt had never been given a fair chance. He also began to write a play based upon one of his short stories. During the summer and autumn of 1954 this play became his main project. He called it *Cat On A Hot Tin Roof*. When he completed the first version he showed it to director Elia Kazan, who had staged *A Streetcar Named Desire* and *Camino Real*. Despite reservations about the final act (which was revised in the Broadway production) Kazan was enthusiastic and took the directing assignment. *Cat On A Hot Tin Roof* opened in March, 1955, to critical and popular acclaim. It garnered Williams his second Pulitzer Prize and reestablished him as one of America's most vital and powerful dramatists.

In 1956 Williams accomplished the feat he had hoped to for sixteen years. He at last brought *Battle Of Angels* to Broadway. Much of it was rewritten and it also had a new title, *Orpheus Descending*, but it remained in essence the same play Williams had written in 1939. Its fate was somewhat better than that of *Battle Of Angels*, but it was neither a critical nor a popular success. Williams was bitterly disappointed. He had invested more of himself in it than in any other play and now it had collapsed a second time. He became gloomy and morose. But the failure of *Orpheus Descending* was not at the core of his depression. Death had struck the Williams family twice in the past two years. In 1955 the Reverend Walter Dakin, Williams' maternal grandfather, died of a stroke. He had lived a long, full life, and his death was not a shock to the playwright, but Williams was deeply saddened. The relationship between the old man and his grandson had been based upon a deep mutual admiration and respect, and the playwright felt his loss keenly. In 1957 Williams' father died in Knoxville, Tennessee. Although the relationship between the father and son had always been strained, Williams was at last able to understand and pity this older man who had misunderstood his family and had been in turn misunderstood by them. The surviving members of the family were now Mrs. Williams, Dakin, a younger brother, and Rose, still incurably ill. The pressures and anxieties resulting from the deaths in his family, from Rose's illness, and from the failures of *Camino Real* and *Orpheus Descending*, plagued Williams throughout 1957. It was out of this oppressive situation that the playwright wrote *Suddenly Last Summer*, a one-act play which he since stated was a kind of personal catharsis. It was his first play, since a successful revival of *Summer And Smoke*, to be performed Off-Broadway, and it received a substantial run.

Williams followed the success of *Suddenly Last Summer* with *Sweet Bird Of Youth*, which opened on Broadway in March of 1959. The play was an overwhelming popular success and proved to be the most substantial triumph for the playwright since *Cat On A Hot Tin Roof*. By this time Williams' writing for the stage had to share a position of importance with his work in films. Most of his major plays were being made into films and he was busy writing the screenplays for some of them. In 1956 he had written an original screenplay based on three of his short dramas. It was called *Baby Doll* and was made into a highly controversial motion picture.

But the theatre remained Williams' first love and he returned to it enthusiastically. *Period Of Adjustment*, a comedy about marital problems, was produced in 1960. It was followed a year later by *Night Of The Iguana* and in 1962 by *The Milk Train Doesn't Stop Here Anymore*. By the beginning of 1964, Tennessee Williams was working on drafts of two new plays.

On the evening of March 31, 1945, the New York drama critics, along with hundreds of theater enthusiasts, witnessed the arrival of one of America's most promising young playwrights, Tennessee Williams. The opening night of *The Glass Menagerie* did not meet with the unanimous approval of the critics; the memory of a Boston failure, *Battle of Angels* in 1940, was still vividly recalled. But two years later, on December 3, 1947, the expectations of Williams' faithful admirers were undeniably justified when *A Streetcar Named Desire* opened at the Ethel Barrymore Theater in New York City. It was acclaimed as "the most moving American play of the past dozen years." Tennessee Williams' career as a playwright was fully established-but not without anguish and difficulties.

BACKGROUND

He was born Thomas Lanier Williams on March 26, 1911 in the rectory of the Episcopal church in Columbus, Mississippi. His mother, Edwina, was the daughter of a clergyman in Delta County, the Reverend Walter E. Dakin. She was gentle, straitlaced, prim, and vivacious, and romantically attracted to life on the beautiful Southern plantations. She had a strain of Puritanism in her which stood in marked contrast to the dueling-pistol-corn-liquor brand-background of her husband, Cornelius Coffin Williams.

Tennessee's father was a violent, aggressive man with a gruff, booming voice. A descendant of frontiersmen and Indian fighters, he had himself been a lieutenant in the Spanish-American War. This heritage of adventurousness and violence fused with his mother's romanticism and Southern gentility seems to have determined the conflict of emotions expressed in Williams' plays.

When he met Edwina Dakin, Cornelius Williams was working for the telephone company in Memphis. Shortly after their marriage, he became a travelling shoe salesman for the International Shoe Company. Since he was always on the road, his wife was compelled to return to her family in Mississippi. Thus young Tom spent the first eight years of his life, along with his mother and his older sister Rose, under the influence and tutelage of his beloved grandfather, Reverend Dakin.

EARLY YEARS IN MISSISSIPPI

Life in the Columbian rectory was rather sheltered, but Tom loved to tag along after his grandfather on parish calls and listen to the conversations. At the age of five, young Williams became ill with diphtheria, the first of many illnesses. During his convalescent period he was very much pampered by his mother, who read to him constantly. His grandfather, who was "crazy" about Edgar Allan Poe and macabre stories, recited poetry to him. This early exposure to literature developed a strong interest in reading and a rich imagination, but Williams' many illnesses also made him a hypochondriac, and he remained delicate and shy. During these years, his sister Rose was his constant companion. He regarded her as a symbol of loveliness.

YEARS IN ST LOUIS

In 1918, when Williams was eight years old, his family moved to St. Louis, Missouri, to join his father who had been promoted to sales manager of a branch office. But the close union of father and son proved disastrous. Cornelius Williams was a man with a strong masculine personality, and he found it difficult to accept his quiet, sensitive son. He tried to encourage Tom in baseball and other virile activities, but young Williams' inability to conform to his father's demands led the latter to denounce him as "sissified." Tom regarded such treatment with bitter resentment and withdrew further into a world of feminine companionship, his mother and his sister Rose.

Life in St. Louis was tainted with bitterness and resentment for the younger Williams. He found it difficult to adjust to living in small, shabby apartments, a necessity caused by his father's refusal to support the family adequately. He hated the school he attended because of the ridicule and abuse he received from the other boys. Only in the presence of his sister Rose, and the little world of unreality they built together, was life tolerable.

Rose, too, was affected by the move to St. Louis. She was entering puberty, but due to the lack of a stable family life, she was unable to make the transition successfully. Filled with fear and anxiety, Rose became mentally ill, finding it totally impossible to communicate with the world of reality. Thus

Thomas Williams was left alone in a world of reality which he did not enjoy. To find his escape, he turned to writing.

BEGINNING OF A WRITING CAREER

When he was twelve, Mrs. Williams presented her son with a gift of a ten-dollar typewriter. Sitting behind the typewriter in the solitude of his small and lonely room. Tennessee found it possible to forget his uncomfortable connection with the outside world. The moment he began writing, he found not only a satisfaction, but a desperate need for the means of expression it offered him.

Recognition first came to Williams as the result of writing contests. He won his first prize of $24 in a contest sponsored by a Southern women's poetry club. While in high school, he received $35 for a story titled "The Vengeance of Nitocris" when it was sold to the Magazine, *Weird Tales*. For answering the question "Can a Good Wife Be a Good Sport," a publication called *Smart Set* awarded him $25. Ironically, he also received recognition from his father, who believed the success of a job was measured by its monetary value.

Writing became part of Williams' daily routine. He wrote poems, stories, film reviews, and contest essays. After finishing high school, he entered the University of Missouri as a major in journalism. Within two years, Williams realized his interest in writing did not include the recording of news. Bored with his studies, he became involved in fraternity life and neglected his classes. His grades fell. When his father discovered that he had failed a course in R.O.T.C., he forced Williams to withdraw from school.

FROM CLERK TO PLAYWRIGHT

The Great Depression of 1929 was now in full swing. As a practical man, Corneluis Williams entered his son in the world of business. Williams became a clerk in the shoe factory that employed his father. He was totally unsuited for the job, but persisted in it for two years. His only means of escape from the drudgery of his meaningless employment were his evenings of writing. Night after night, when supper was finished, he would go to his room and type until three or four o'clock in the morning. At six o'clock in the morning, his mother would call him with the familiar "Rise and shine, rise and shine," as Amanda does in *The Glass Menagerie*. When she opened his door, she usually found him lying across his bed, still fully clothed. Two years later Williams was back with his grandparents at their new home in Memphis, recuperating from a nervous breakdown. An excess of coffee, cigarettes, and long hours of writing had broken his health, but had liberated him from the monotony of the shoe factory.

INTEREST IN DRAMA

During his period of convalescence in Memphis in the summer of 1935, Williams was introduced, for the first time, to drama. He wrote a play for the Rose Arbor little-theater group called, *Cairo! Shanghai! Bombay!* For the audience, the play-about the adventures of two sailors on shore leave-was a moderate success. For Williams, the discovery of the thrill of people responding to his work confirmed him in the belief that the theater was the medium that would make use of his best efforts.

On his return to St. Louis, he continually sought outlets for his newly discovered interest. He became a member of a group of young poets headed by a poet called Clark Mills. This association proved invaluable in his formative years. Through it, he became acquainted with the works of Anton Chekhov, Herman Melville, Rainer Maria Rilke, D. H. Lawrence, and Hart Crane-his greatest poetic idol.

FOUR PLAYS AND "THE MUMMERS"

Under the influence of such literary greats, he wrote his second play, *The Magic Tower*, which was produced in 1936 by a little-theater group in Webster Groves, Missouri. He then became associated with a small theatrical group in St. Louis called the "Mummers." Williams was greatly stimulated by this small acting group which, he says, was "a disorderly theater group of St. Louis, standing socially, if not artistically, opposite to the usual Little Theater groups." They produced three of the playwright's works; *Headlines*, a one-act play denouncing compulsory military training, used as a curtain raiser for Irwin Shaw's play, *Bury The Dead*; *Candles to the Sun*, a full length drama depicting the life and despair of the laboring population in an Alabama mining camp; and *Fugitive Kind*, a character study of destitute men in the slums of St. Louis.

While writing plays for the Mummers, Williams had the opportunity to develop a fuller understanding of the theater. He grew sensitive to the use of light, music, and theatrical effects. He had always been attracted to a world of make-believe, but not without a sense of guilt; it had remained for him an escape when the pressures of reality were too great. In the theater, Williams discovered the means of treating reality through a kind of make-believe, using symbolism and poetic language.

A LOST CONTEST

During his association with the Mummers, Williams enrolled as a senior at Washington University, St. Louis. In one of his classes, playwriting, each student was to submit a one-act play at the end of the year to be judged in competition for a $50 prize. Williams' entry was a play about a World War I munitions manufacturer who sold his products to the highest bidder: *Me, Vashya*. Encouraged by the success of his work with the Mummers, Williams fully expected to win the contest. When his name did not appear among the winners, he reacted violently; it was a humiliation which he could not endure. He terminated his association with the University before the end of the year.

FAMILY PROBLEMS

But Williams' interest in writing persisted, as did his concern for the difficulties in his life at home. His mother and father were constantly quarrelling, and he often became the object of his father's vindictiveness. Cornelius Williams loved the adventure of a salesman's life on the road; it was difficult for him to adjust to a sedentary home life. Unlike his son, whose world was enriched through his creative imagination, he found his means of escape in drinking and playing poker in the company of other salesmen. He remained alien to the needs and interests of his family. Edwina Williams, conditioned by the necessity of raising a virtually fatherless family, became dominating and demanding.

The strife of this unsettled homelife took its major toll on Rose, Tom's sister. Her gentleness and sensitivity were crushed under the pressure of her mother's domination. Her father was a stranger to her, who barged in and out of her life with no real meaning. She was embarrassed when Tom, at his mother's insistence, brought home "gentleman callers," as Tom Wingfield does in *The Glass Menagerie*. Her mother usually dressed Rose in old-fashioned Southern costumes; she looked lovely, but she never talked-her mother never gave her a chance. She found no release for her pent-up emotions. In 1937, Rose was committed to an asylum for the insane.

Williams was greatly affected by the loss of his sister. His distress at his inability to help her and the memory of her helplessness are hauntingly echoed in *The Glass Menagerie*.

THE ROAD TO SUCCESS

In the fall of 1937, Williams, determined to complete his college education, enrolled in the University of Iowa. Finding a theatrical environment that suited him, he was encouraged to write two plays. *Spring Storm* was composed for a seminar in playwriting conducted by the late Professor E. C. Mabie. It is a play which has been praised for its dialogue and atmosphere, but is considered to be of no great value. Williams considers the second play, *Not About Nightingales*, to be the best of his early efforts. It was a play that dealt with horror and violence, using for its plot an actual incident that occurred in a prison at that time.

BOHEMIAN LIFE

By the spring of 1938, Williams had managed to finish his college career at the University of Iowa and received his degree as a Bachelor of Arts. Upon graduating, his immediate concern was earning a living. But Chicago was a hard place to do this, for it was still feeling the effects of the Depression. He applied for a job with the W.P.A. Writers' Project, but was refused because he was unable to prove that his family was in need of financial help. Returning to St. Louis, he found nothing but his father's insistence that he go back to work in the shoe factory.

Having tasted the fruits of freedom, he rebelled against the attempt to draw him back into the web of family ties. He escaped once again and landed in the midst of an artist's oasis, New Orleans. The life of a Bohemian was much to his liking and he adopted its ways without any apparent difficulty. Still in need of money, he was content to work as a waiter in a twenty-five-cents-a-meal restaurant. By day, he was a simple, honest table tender, but at night he was a poet. He walked the streets of New Orleans with an adventurous soul, a clear mind, and a sensitive memory. When he returned to his room, he wrote about the brave, the frightened, the pure, the corrupt, the angry, the gentle, the clear, the confused, and the creative people of his newly discovered world. During this period, he lived near street-car tracks on which two cars, one named Desire and the other named Cemetery, would complete their daily rounds. To him they seemed to symbolize the nature of life in the French Quarter, and he filed the idea in his memory for future creative use.

FROM THOMAS TO TENNESSEE

When Williams emerged from New Orleans for the first time, he was a changed person. Even his name was different. He adopted the nickname given to him by his classmates at Washington University: "Tennessee." He headed for California in a 1934 Ford, accompanied by a clarinet player and former teacher, James Parrott. The trip was not without event. They ran out of gas as well as money. The problem of gas was quickly solved by siphoning it from unattended cars; money remained a problem for quite some time. Occasionally, there was slight relief in the form of letters from Williams' grandmother to which a $10 bill would be attached.

Before leaving New Orleans, Williams had read an article announcing a playwriting contest sponsored by the New York Group Theatre. He had submitted four full-length plays and a group of one-actors called *American Blues* to be judged by Harold Clurman, Irwin Shaw, and Molly Day Thatcher (Mrs. Elia Kazan). One day, while he was living in California, badly in need of funds, he received a telegram announcing that he had won the $100 prize for his one-actors.

AN AGENT AND A GRANT

In addition to this stroke of good luck, one of the more important events in his life took place. Through the recommendation of Molly Day Thatcher, Audrey Wood, her very good friend and a noted New York literary agent, consented to handle the work of Tennessee Williams. With a sincere interest in the development of the young playwright, Audrey Wood set out to obtain financial assistance from the Rockefeller Foundation. She was successful in getting a grant of $1,000, enabling Williams to continue writing on a new full-length play. It was the *Battle of Angels*.

The New School for Social Research also became interested in the talent of this young playwright and awarded Williams a scholarship which enabled him to come to New York and work under the guidance of John Gassner and Theresa Helburn. With the help of these two associates of the Theatre Guild, *Battle of Angels* was scheduled for a premier performance in New York in 1941 to become Williams' first Broadway play.

"BATTLE OF ANGELS"

The play went into rehearsal in the fall of 1940. It had all the earmarks of success, with producer Lawrence Langner and director Margaret Webster to guide the production. Miriam Hopkins was signed for the leading role of Myra Torrence. The play, however, contained flaws which were difficult to overcome, even with the help of a polished Broadway production. After seeing the first draft, John Gassner had awarded the play with the distinction of being the best script he had seen in five years. Williams, however, made revisions which were very ill-advised, and the final script evolved as an inferior product.

The play opened for its out-of-town tryout in Boston on December 30, 1940. Shortly after the curtain had opened, the audience reacted adversely to the display of religion and sex combined in a potpourri of misplaced symbols and violence. When the moment for the **climax** in Act Three arrived, the stage manager, who had been warned of an insufficient amount of smoke for the burning scene, let loose with a billow of smoke that overwhelmed the audience as well as the stage. This was hardly noticed however, as most of the audience had left long before the third-act curtain had parted. After being denounced by the Watch and Ward Society of Boston, the Theatre Guild sent an unprecedented letter of apology to its subscribers and closed the play. The results were catastrophic, but after the smoke had cleared, it was undeniable that a new playwright had made himself known.

TOWARD A DARK REALITY

Completely discouraged by his first experience with professional theater, Tennessee Williams again became the restless, wandering writer. He returned to New Orleans, and with the help of a second Rockefeller grant and royalties from his one-act plays, he escaped back into his own world of reality-writing. He wrote poems and short stories and sent them to small literary magazines. Feeling an initial fondness for his first Broadway attempt, he worked on revising *Battle of Angels*.

Williams grew obsessed with the need for expressing basic reality. His experience in Boston made him conscious of the fact that people rebel against the more sordid aspect of life.

In the face of this adversity, however, he tended to emphasize the unsavory details.

His new plays reflected this attitude: *Portrait of a Madonna* and *The Lady of the Larkspur Lotion* both show the degeneracy of the young Southern belle turned prostitute (later to be seen as the character of Blanche Du Bois in *A Streetcar Named Desire*); *Lord Byron's Love Letter* deals with a lamented love affair between Lord Byron and the woman who bore his illegitimate child; the story, *One Arm*, reveals the life of a male prostitute who murders a male client; an incident of incest and the violation of Spanish honor was told in *The Purification*; and the story *Twenty-seven Wagons Full of Cotton* (which became the film *Baby Doll*) concerned a cotton farmer's wife who has an affair with a neighbor while the husband is out ginning the neighbor's cotton. Other stories and plays appeared with the same type of thematic material. But even if one were to object to Williams' plots, admiration must be expressed for his ability to write dialogue, portray character, establish mood, and arouse the interest of an audience.

BACK TO NEW YORK

In 1942, Williams left New Orleans and travelled to Mexico where he commenced work on a full-length play called *Stairs To The Roof*-about a clerk in a shirt factory who escapes from the drudgery of his job by climbing the stairs to the roof of the store to smoke. Williams then returned to New York, where he managed to subsist by working at various odd jobs: waiting on tables in a restaurant; ushering in the Strand Theater; operating an elevator; and reciting poetry in a Greenwich Village bar. He also managed to collaborate with a friend, Donald Windham, on a play called *You Touched Me*. It was a comedy-patterned after a story by D. H. Lawrence-which appeared on Broadway three years later.

IN AND OUT OF HOLLYWOOD

Williams continued to write, but when the money from the Rockefeller grant ran out, he became desperate. Audrey Wood came to his aid again and sent him to Hollywood as a script writer for M.G.M. The pay was good-$250 a week-but Williams found it impossible to work in a celluloid world of make-believe. He soon managed to get fired with the unanimous agreement of his employers. While still on the payroll of M.G.M., Williams worked out the synopsis for a film he titled *The Gentleman Caller*. After it was rejected by the studio, he changed it to a stage play and renamed it *The Glass Menagerie*.

WRITING "THE GLASS MENAGERIE"

This play was a departure from Williams' usual style. It was more delicate, more sympathetic, and more lyrical than any of his other plays. In it, he looked at life objectively and showed tolerance and understanding. Perhaps his experience with the film industry of working at a fairly decent salary caused him to be less bitter. The days Williams spent on writing *The Glass Menagerie* were the happiest in years. At the time he was released from his contract at M.G.M., he was told to draw his pay quietly for three and a half months, but to stay away from the office. He spent the remainder of this time on the beach at Santa Monica, relaxed and in good health.

PRODUCTION OF "MENAGERIE"

Audrey Wood was much impressed by Williams new play and took plans to find a sympathetic producer. Her choice was producer-director-actor Eddie Dowling, who immediately took an option on the play. Shortly after, the show went into rehearsal with an enthusiastic cast. Julie Haydon took the part of Laura on the advice of her husband, George Jean Nathan. Laurette Taylor, considered to be America's greatest living actress, came out of retirement to play Amanda. Dowling reserved the role of Tom for himself and cast Anthony Ross in the part of the Gentleman Caller.

But rehearsals did not proceed smoothly. Differences of opinion regarding interpretation, direction of stage business, ability of other actors, etc, became points of grievance. When the show moved to Chicago for its out-of-town tryout, difficulties with the set and costumes plagued the production. Nevertheless, when the curtain parted on the opening night, everything fell into place. The critics raved about the play, with minor exceptions, and hailed Miss Taylor as having equaled her greatest role. Although the reviews were good, the public was slow in responding. Displeased by the small audiences, the critics began to print a steady stream of propaganda to encourage attendance. The publicity helped. Gradually attendance grew, and within three weeks, the play became a popular success.

On opening night in New York, March 31, 1945, *The Glass Menagerie* was received with the same amount of enthusiasm by both the critics and the public. Box office business grew and the show enjoyed a two-year run on Broadway. When the critics met on the 10th of April, they chose the play for the 1945 Critics' Award.

TO "STREETCAR" AND A PULITZER PRIZE

With the jinx of Broadway now broken, Williams showed more confidence in his work. The only moderate success of his collaboration with Donald Windham, *You Touched Me*, which appeared on Broadway six months after Menagerie, did very little to dampen his spirits. The theater world was waiting for further proof of the new young playwright's talent, and Williams was preparing for the challenge.

He began work on a play he called *The Poker Night*, but while travelling from New York to Mexico-a move he felt was necessary to finish his work-Williams became ill with a ruptured appendix. Being a confirmed hypochondriac, he believed the ailment to be much worse than the doctor's diagnosis had determined. Although the operation was a success, Williams convalesced with the belief that his next play would be his last. He worked diligently on his new play, pouring into it all of his energy and talent.

By 1947 the play was completed, and he renamed it *A Streetcar Named Desire*. It was truly a masterpiece. It appeared on Broadway under the guiding hands of one of the Theater's ablest directors, Elia Kazan. Jessica Tandy played Blanche-Williams' finest creation-and Stanley was played by a lesser-known talent, Marlon Brando. When the play opened in New York in December 3, 1974, it was immediately a resounding success; the critics were unanimous in their praise; Williams was established as one of America's greatest playwrights. That year, in addition to receiving the Critics' Award, he received for the first time, the Pulitzer Prize.

"SUMMER AND SMOKE"

But *Streetcar* was not Tennessee Williams' last play as he had predicted. His health continued in excellent condition as he worked to complete yet another script-for a play titled *Summer and Smoke*. Unfortunately, it was completed while *Streetcar* was still in popular demand at the box office. When it opened on Broadway, October 6, 1948, the critics considered *Summer and Smoke* an anticlimax in the development of Williams' talent. It had a moderate run on Broadway and then faded into the shadows of its more successful predecessor. But it was to emerge once more at a more favorable time-in an off-Broadway theater under the direction of Jose Quintero-to become the most highly acclaimed off-Broadway production of 1952.

"CAMINO REAL"

Williams, disappointed with his failure of 1948, left New York and travelled to Europe. Rome impressed him greatly. While there, he felt encouraged to finish an old one-act play, *Camino Real*. In *Camino Real*, he attempted to create his own type of reality through a strangely fashioned, symbolistic world.

As Williams forged ahead to explain life in terms of symbols, characters, and favorite phrases, the audience was left behind in a world of fantasy. The 1953 failure of this play on Broadway left the author with bitter resentment, but it was an experience from which he benefited greatly. His next play showed the results of an imposed discipline and a return to objective reality.

ITALY AND "THE ROSE TATTOO"

The warmth and sweetness of the Italian people showed Williams an entirely new philosophy of living. After meeting one of Italy's most talented actresses, Anna Magnani, he was inspired to write *The Rose Tattoo*. The play was not a success when it opened on Broadway in February 1951. The critics were impressed by a rich and lyric portrait of an Italian peasant, but the Latin way of life was still foreign to the author. This fact also was evident in the writing of a novel, *The Roman Spring of Mrs. Stone*, which came from William's typewriter around the same time as *The Rose Tattoo*.

"CAT ON A HOT TIN ROOF"

The play was developed from a short story called Three Players of a Summer Game. Williams worked for several years to adapt his short story to a full-length play. With the failure of *Camino Real*, the author felt a strong compulsion to justify his writing talents. When *Cat on a Hot Tin Roof* opened on Broadway on March 24, 1955, not only was the author reassured of a successfully maturing talent, but the audience was assured of the author's ability to create understandable situations and people.

TWO DEATHS AND DISAPPOINTMENT

The year 1955 brought Williams his third Critics' Award and his second Pulitzer Prize, but it was also a year that brought a deep personal loss-the death of Williams' beloved grandfather, Reverend Walter Dakin. After his wife's death in 1944, Walter Dakin had agreed to live with his grandson. For several years, he accompanied the young playwright from New York to Florida, and they became a very devoted pair. Although Reverend Dakin lived a long and full life-he was ninety-eight when he died-Williams was deeply affected by his death.

Williams returned to his work, intent upon revising some of his earlier plays, but it brought nothing but disappointment. When the film script for *Baby Doll*, constructed from his one-act play, *Twenty-Seven Wagons Full of Cotton*, appeared on the screen, it was denounced as being one of the most unhealthy and amoral pictures ever made in this country. One last attempt at revising the script of *Battle of Angels* resulted (in 1957) in another failure-called *Orpheus Descending*.

That same year brought the death of his father, Cornelius Williams, a man for whom the playwright had found very little sympathy while he was living. But after his father's death, Williams expressed understanding and pity for the man, whom, he said, he no longer "hates."

"SUDDENLY LAST SUMMER"

Through all the feelings of disappointment for his professional failures, grief for the lost members of his family, and guilt for the helpless mental condition of his sister, Williams continued to write. His new play was the most shocking of his career, a one-actor called *Suddenly Last Summer*. It appeared off-Broadway with another of his one-act plays, *Something Unspoken*. The entire evening was titled *Garden District* because of its scenic location in the garden district of New Orleans. Ironically, the play won praise from the critics. Williams was called "the poet of the damned" who "denied the values by which most people lived" in the "horrible beauty of his dreadful speeches."

With such distinction to his credit, he dug deep into his psychological concerns and came up with *Sweet Bird of Youth*. All seven of the New York drama critics found praise for the play on its opening night in March of 1959.

Since then, businessmen have considered Tennessee Williams a safe investment for the future. His stock value dropped slightly in November 1960 after the opening of *Period of Adjustment*. But when *Night of the Iguana* opened late in December of 1961, Williams proved to be in his best dramatic form since *Streetcar*. The play won for him his fourth Critics' Circle Award.

THE REBEL ESTABLISHED

Despite the complete failure in 1962 of *The Milk Train Doesn't Stop Here Anymore*, Williams remains established as one of America's most successful playwrights. He has also written poems, short stories, a novel, a libretto for an opera, and many screen adaptations of his plays. Tennessee Williams will continue to write for anyone who is willing to watch and listen.

His influence in the American Theater has been monumental. As the "fool" that walked "where angels fear to tread," he has helped to create an atmosphere of freedom for up-and-coming playwrights. He has educated modern theater audiences through the use of embarrassment and anger. His technique has not always been appreciated, but he has awakened an interest in theatre in a public that now accepts the works of Ionesco, Beckett, Genet, Pinter, and others of the new Avant Garde school of playwriting. The American Theater has a great deal to be thankful for in the works of Tennessee Williams.

THE GLASS MENAGERIE

TEXTUAL ANALYSIS

PART 1

CHARACTERS

Amanda Wingfield-the mother. Laura Wingfield-her daughter. Tom Wingfield-her son and the narrator of the play. Jim O'Connor-the gentleman caller.

SETTING

An alley and the Wingfield apartment in St. Louis.

Time: 1945 and the past.

ACT I: SCENE 1

The Curtain Opens

The scene opens on a dimly lit stage, which reflects the mood of the play: "memory." Because it is a "memory play," a good bit of poetic license can be taken with regard to detail: in some cases it is omitted, and in some cases it is exaggerated to meet the emotional demands of the play's theme.

Through the darkness, the audience sees the back of a building which later reveals itself to be the transparent wall of the Wingfield apartment. The apartment faces an alley and is entered by the use of a fire escape. It is by way of this alley that the exterior entrances and exits of the various characters are made. The interior of the apartment is divided into two areas: the living room and the dining room. In the living room are located a chair, a sofa (which unfolds to become Laura's bed), a phonograph, and an old-fashioned what-not table that contains a number of transparent glass animals. On the wall hangs a picture of the father with an infectious, enduring smile on his face.

Tom Appears

Through the initial darkness of the opening moments of the play, comes a figure dressed as a merchant seaman. He strolls to the center of the top platform of the fire escape and lights a cigarette. As the cigarette ignites, the play begins.

Comment

It is very important for the reader to become aware of the atmosphere established in the opening sequence of the play. A mood is created, which is ever-present through the entire play. Williams tells us that his play is "non-realistic." The truth of the play lies not in what the audience sees, but in the way the audience relates what they see to incidents that have happened in their own lives.

Tom as the Narrator

It becomes apparent that the figure in the seaman's cap and jacket is Tom Wingfield. He is the narrator of the play and also one of the important characters in the drama which is about to unfold. He addresses the audience directly, setting the stage for the drama by taking the audience back into the past. He recalls days when he was younger and gazed at life from the back alley of a St. Louis tenement building. As the narrator, Tom speaks with the perspective of time. He depicts the days of the depression era as characterized by a dissolving economy, labor disturbances, and revolutions in foreign countries: "That is the social background of this play."

He then becomes more specifically related to the other characters in the drama. He introduces his mother, Amanda; his sister, Laura; and a gentleman caller, Jim O'Connor, whom he calls the most realistic character in the play. His father is a missing member of the family who appears only as a picture hanging on the wall. He was a father who became disenchanted by the pressures and obligations of family life, and "skipped the light fantastic out of town."

Comment

Notice the similarity between Tom and his father in their need to escape from family obligations.

The Action Starts

As Amanda is heard talking to Laura at the dining room table, Tom's image fades. He appears again as the younger Tom, seated at the table eating breakfast. Tom's relationship with his mother becomes immediately apparent. She commences to badger him by criticizing his eating habits. She explains that animals can swallow food whole, but human beings must "chew, chew, chew." Tom soon relinquishes his attempts to eat a satisfying meal, and escapes into the living room for a quiet smoke, only to become the victim of Amanda's criticism of smoking. Laura attempts to divert the tension between Amanda and Tom by offering to serve the coffee.

Now Laura becomes the victim. Amanda insists that Laura rest and prepare herself for her gentleman callers. Amanda relates an incident in her youth, at her childhood home in Blue Mountain on the Mississippi Delta, when seventeen gentleman callers dropped in unexpectedly. This is an incident that she has told her children many times. As Amanda interrupts her story to go for the coffee, Tom expresses his irritation at the story's repetition. Laura pleads with him for patience, saying: "she loves to tell it."

Amanda's Disappointment

Amanda returns and continues to tell about her life as a young girl with a pretty face, a graceful figure, and "a nimble wit and a tongue to meet all occasions." A youthful gleam comes into her eyes as she recalls the many opportunities she had to marry some of the most prominent men on the Mississippi Delta. The gleam fades as she turns to the smiling picture on the wall and exclaims, "But-what did I do? I just went out of my way and picked your father."

Comment

Amanda expresses her own disappointment in this reflection of the startling contrast between her childhood dreams and what has actually happened to her life.

Amanda, again, insists that Laura keep fresh and pretty for her gentleman callers. Laura, embarrassed and hurt by her mother's innocent but errant attentions, feebly tries to explain that she is not expecting any gentleman callers. The scene ends with Laura standing is a fading light, admitting to Tom: "Mother's afraid that I'm going to be an old maid."

ACT I: SCENE 2

Laura's Deception

As the scene opens, we find Laura alone on the stage. She is kneeling next to the menagerie and is polishing and tending to the glass animals with great care. In the background we hear the phonograph playing one of the old, worn-out dance records left to her by her father. Laura is lost in a world of make-believe. Suddenly, Amanda appears at the door. Upon hearing her, Laura quickly returns the pieces of glass to their place on the table and seats herself at a typewriter. She is typing as Amanda enters.

Amanda pauses as she sees Laura. A look of hopelessness and despair is reflected in her face. Then, in a sudden burst of anger, she crosses the room toward Laura. Grabbing the typing charts, she tears them and throws them to the floor. Laura becomes rigid with fright. Amanda, now humiliated and embarrassed, tells Laura that she is aware of her deception. She relates how, on her way to a D.A.R. meeting, Amanda visited the business school where Laura was enrolled, to check on her progress. At first, the teacher did not recognize the name. Then she recalled that a terribly shy little girl dropped out of school shortly after the class began: on a day when the class was to take a speed test, the girl became ill and had to be carried from the room; she never returned. Amanda tells Laura how the teacher took out the attendance record to verify the facts of her story, and there was the name, Laura Wingfield.

Laura, affected by her mother's grave disappointment, admits that she had not attended school. She tells Amanda how she would leave the house every morning at half past seven and just walk. Sometimes she would visit the museum of the birdhouses at the zoo, or go to the movies. Despondently, Amanda warns Laura of the dangers of becoming an unmarried spinster unable to cope with life, like the "Little birdlike women without any nest eating the crust of humility all their lives."

Comment

At this point we realize that Amanda's interest in Laura's future is sincere. She is aware of the cruel blows that life can wield. Because of her delicate nature, Laura would find facing life alone a terrible hardship. Amanda's one remaining hope is to find a young man for Laura.

"Blue Roses"

Laura mentions that she once liked a boy she met in high school; his name was Jim. He was very popular with the students and sang the lead in the senior class operetta, "The Pirates of Penzance." She met Jim while attending a class they had together. He used to call her "Blue Roses," because of the time she had to stay out of school with an attack of pleurosis. As Amanda realizes that Laura was fond of Jim, her one remaining hope begins to kindle into a burning desire. She is not even disappointed to hear of Jim's probable marriage. Amanda decides to see that Laura ends up married to a very nice young man.

Laura reminds her mother that she is a cripple, but Amanda will not be daunted. She reassures Laura that a slight disadvantage like that can be overcome with charm. "That's the only thing your father had plenty of-charm."

ACT I: SCENE 3

Amanda's Plans

Tom reappears as the narrator and recalls how his mother became obsessed with the anticipated arrival of the gentleman caller. His image became the hope for the future, a goal toward which every member of the family must strive. Amanda planned his arrival as meticulously as an invading general plans an attack. To earn the extra money she wants to make the home more presentable to the intended visitor, she solicits telephone subscriptions to a magazine called "The Homemaker's Companion."

The scene then shifts to the interior of the Wingfield apartment. Several months have passed; it is now early Spring. Amanda is talking on the telephone. During her conversation, Tom enters, seats himself at the dining room table, and begins to write. He is barely visible in the dull glow of a table lamp. Laura is seated in the living room. Amanda's telephone conversation is cut of abruptly.

Comment

Amanda's two telephone conversations at the beginning of **Act I: Scene 3** and the end of **Act I: Scene 5** can prove to be high points in Amanda's characterization, if handled properly by the actress. They show capsule expressions of Amanda's ability to cope with disappointment and with joy. In **Scene 3**, she is refused a subscription renewal when the intended subscriber mentions the need to check the oven to prevent her dinner from burning and hangs up on Amanda. Amanda feels the disappointment, but is capable of dismissing it with a slight shrug and a nervous laugh. (**Scene 5** will be discussed later.)

Amanda Harasses Tom

As Amanda hangs up the phone, the light in the living room and dining room become brighter. Amanda, seeking relief from her embarrassment, talks with Laura. Not wanting to disturb Tom, Laura mentions to her mother that he is trying to write. Amanda, still affected by the telephone call, nervously starts adjusting the table lamp for Tom in order to save his eyesight. Tom tries to object, but Amanda continues, telling him that he must sit up straight because "your stomach presses against your lungs, and your lungs press against your heart, and that poor little heart gets discouraged because it hasn't got any room left to go on beating."

Tom becomes furious. Writing and reading were the only activities left that he could call his own. Now his mother was imposing on his private life too. Just yesterday she took one of his books back to the library-"that awful book by that insane Mr. Lawrence-I won't allow such filth in my house." Tom tells Amanda that he also has a life to live. Amanda accuses Tom of being selfish. Tom, infuriated, explains that he is working in the warehouse of a shoe factory, a job he loathes, and that for sixty-five dollars a month he is giving up all that he has dreamed of doing and ever being.

Comment

This conformation between Amanda and Tom is one of the major dramatic moments of the play. For the first time Tom openly and forcefully declares his true feelings about his bleak home life existence. He does this with abandonment-as would anyone who has been pushed over the brink of tolerance-and with the intention to hurt his adversary. However, the greatest dramatic effect does not come from the verbal dual between Amanda and Tom, but rather from seeing the fragile and incompetent figure of Laura against the unstable world that is yet her only security.

Anger and Accident

Tom grabs his jacket and heads for the door. Amanda stops him with a demand to know where he is going. Tom answers defiantly: "I'm going to the movies." Amanda considers this a lie. Tom takes advantage of her disbelief and taunts his mother by telling her he leads a double life: "By day I'm a simple, honest warehouse worker, but at night I'm a dynamic czar of the underworld." He relates dramatically how he runs dens of vice and iniquity, and that he has many enemies who plan on destroying him: "some night they're going to blow us sky-high, and will I be happy! And so will you be. You'll go up-up-over Blue Mountain on a broomstick! With seventeen gentleman callers. You ugly babbling old witch."

Tom grabs his jacket and starts to put it on as he heads for the door. His hand gets caught in the sleeve, he whips around and throws the jacket into the room. It hits the glass menagerie and a shattering of glass is heard Laura cries out. Tom stands, stunned by the realization of what he has accidentally done to Laura. Amanda tells him that she will never speak to him again and walks out. But he does not hear his mother's parting curse, and walks slowly and penitently towards Laura. As he reaches the menagerie, he kneels to pick up the pieces of broken glass animals. He is unable to speak as the scene ends.

ACT I: SCENE 4

The Magician's Escape

The scene opens on a darkened stage. One faint light illuminates the austere outline of the alley. It is five o'clock in the morning, as evidenced by the chiming of a nearby church bell. The unsteady figure of Tom is seen weaving its way down the alley. He responds to each chime of the clock with a violent rattle from a New Year's Eve type of noise maker. His actions indicate that he has been drinking. As he approaches the fire escape, he searches aimlessly for his key. He discovers the key and heads for the door, but before he can fit the key into the lock, it slips through his fingers and falls.

As he lights a match to look for the key, the interior of the apartment brightens. Laura, having heard the noise, comes to the door. As she opens it she finds Tom, down on all fours, looking through a crack in the fire escape. In response to Laura's questions, Tom tells her that he was returning from an all-night movie. There also was a stage show which featured "Malvolio the Magician." One of his tricks was to turn water into whiskey. Tom knows it was whiskey, because he volunteered to taste it "both shows."

Laura assists Tom to the sofa, now unfolded as a bed. As Tom slips off his shoes and lies down to rest he tells Laura that the featured trick of the evening was when the magician allowed himself to be nailed into a coffin and then got out without removing one nail. As the light on the scene dims we hear Tom muttering, "It don't take much intelligence to get yourself into a nailed-up coffin-but who in hell ever got himself out of one without removing one nail?" The light dims, but there is a remaining glow on the smiling face in the picture hanging on the wall.

Comment

In most productions of *The Glass Menagerie*, a light is fastened inside the frame just behind the father's picture. Although the father never appears, when the picture lights up, it becomes symbolic of his continuing influence over the family. The light on the picture glows at this moment of the drama to indicate that Tom's father also escaped from a situation similar to a nailed-up coffin.

ACT I: SCENE 5

This scene begins immediately following **Scene 4**. In the darkness, six chimes ring from the church tower, followed by the insistent ringing of an alarm clock. Then we hear Amanda's morning call: "Rise and shine." Tom's short night's sleep has come to an end.

A Reconciliation

Laura enters from the dining room on her way out to do some shopping. As she passes Tom, she stops for a moment and beseeches him to speak to Amanda and to apologize for his behavior of yesterday. Tom gives her no answer. On her way down the fire escape, Laura trips and falls. Tom, hearing Laura's cry, rushes to the door as Amanda comes in anxiously from the dining room. Laura, embarrassed by the confusion she has caused, quickly recovers and hurries away up the alley.

Amanda and Tom meet, face to face, on the fire escape landing. Amanda deliberately ignores Tom as she walks into the apartment and exits through the dining room to the kitchen. As Tom enters the apartment, Amanda re-enters from the dining room with a tray filled with a bowl of cereal, a coffee cup, and a pot of coffee. She silently indicates to Tom that he should sit and eat. Finally, Tom, feeling the necessity of speaking, apologizes to Amanda for his remarks of the previous evening. Amanda tearfully confesses to Tom how her devotion to her family has made her hateful in the eyes of her children, but her strongest wish and desire has been for their success. With genuine repentance, Tom promises his mother he will try to do better in the future, and that he "won't ever become a drunkard."

Comment

Amanda is beginning to sense the similarity between father and son. She is fearful that Tom will follow the ways of his father and attempt to escape the pressures of family life. He is her security and her hope for the future of her family.

An Estrangement

The air is cleared for the moment, and a deep bond is felt between mother and son. Amanda tells Tom that she wishes to speak to him about Laura: Lately Laura seems nervous and moody. But Laura has also told Amanda that she is worried about Tom. She thinks Tom is not happy. Cautiously, Amanda questions Tom about his strange actions in the past few weeks: drinking and staying out late at night. Tom, affected by his mother's sincere interest, tries to explain to her his feeling toward life-his ambitions, his need for freedom and adventure. But it soon becomes obvious that mother and son have lost their means of communication. Amanda registers no understanding of the feelings Tom tries to express.

Amanda tells Tom that she is aware of his interest in joining the Merchant Marine. She expects that soon, he will be wanting to leave. She is willing to agree to this, "but not till there's somebody to take your place." Amanda insists that until Laura has someone to take care of her, until she is married and has a home of her own, she will not let Tom leave. Amanda tells Tom that she is not concerned for herself, but Laura must become "independent!"

When Tom asks what can be done, Amanda suggests that Tom invite one of his friends at the warehouse home for dinner some night to meet Laura. Tom is embarrassed, but realizing that arguing with Amanda would prove useless, he agrees. As Tom leaves hurriedly, fearing to be late for work, Amanda responds with joy and triumph. She crosses to the telephone with renewed determination and becomes successful in selling a magazine subscription.

Comment

This scene shows the tremendous strength displayed in the character of Amanda. From the moment her husband "fell in love with long distance" and left her, she has been obligated to face life in all its adversity. She has faced it like a man, but in a woman's guise, not expecting a great deal, but always with a plan in mind. When Tom finally acted on her subtle but constant suggestion to bring home a gentleman caller for Laura, Amanda reacts in a typically feminine way. She was joyous, not for her own selfish benefit, but for Laura, whose future happiness is an important concern for the family.

ACT I: SCENE 6

Theme of the Play

Tom appears again as the narrator, dressed in the merchant seaman's jacket and cap. He is standing in the dimly lit alley, watching the faint flashing of a neon sign coming from the Paradise Dance Hall across the way. The brassy blare of dance music reminiscent of the 1920s is heard in the cool spring evening. Tom recalls the evenings he spent standing on the fire escape landing, watching the young couples dancing and living their lives in tune with the rhythms of a waltz or a tango. But while they were dancing, he notes, the rest of the world was preparing for war.

Comment

The opening narrative to **Scene 6** presents the **theme** of the play. Williams contrasts the basic reality of the times, that is, the unsettling political affairs of the world, with the unrealistic attitude of the people who live on the periphery of life. He indicates that people can and will suffer greatly for their deception: Unless people prepare themselves for the true realities in life, they will be destroyed.

Hopes of a Caller

The music stops and we see Amanda coming from the dining room, calling to Tom. In the meantime, Tom has receded into the shadows and returns as the younger Tom (without the jacket and cap). Tom is smoking on the fire escape landing as Amanda approaches him. In the light of a full moon, they talk about many insignificant things. Finally, Tom, realizing the cause of his mother's anxiety, mentions that he has invited a friend from the warehouse for dinner.

Amanda is taken by surprise, but she recovers quickly and starts making preparations for the visitor's arrival. She is excited and happy as she questions Tom about the young man's character. Tom tells her his name is Jim O'Connor and, as a shipping clerk, he makes eighty-five dollars a month. He is a young man who is interested in self-improvement; he goes to night school to study radio engineering and public speaking. As a result, Amanda sees Jim as a perfect match for Laura.

Tom, sensing the danger involved, cautions his mother against expecting too much from Laura. He realizes that Jim lives in a very different world from that in which Laura leads her fragile and sensitive existence. "Laura lives in a world of little glass animals. She plays old phonograph records-and-that's about all."

Amanda refuses to heed Tom's warning, and as he leaves, she calls the unsuspecting Laura out onto the fire escape landing. She tells Laura to look at the moon over her left shoulder and make a wish. The pale face of Laura looks up questioningly at the moon as Amanda instructs her to wish for "happiness and just a little bit of good fortune."

SUMMARY

In Act I we realize the following points:

1. The "memory play" **convention** is established by Tom appearing as the narrator and addressing himself directly to the audience.

2. A conflict exists between Amanda and Tom. There is an indication that something drastic will take place that will strongly affect their relationship.

3. Laura is the main point of concern within the family. She also acts as a silent arbitrator between Tom and Amanda.

4. There is a similarity between Tom and his father with regard to their position in the family, their responsibility as the major means of financial

support, and their need to escape from a situation to which neither was able to adjust.

5. Amanda lives in two worlds: her pleasant dream of the past, and the drab and demanding world of her present.

6. The father's picture represents his strong and lasting influence over the Wingfield family.

7. Amanda refuses to accept Laura's shortcomings. She has continually pushed Laura into frustrating situations.

8. Laura has a desperate need for the glass menagerie as a means of escape from everyday life.

9. Amanda makes the decision to find a husband for Laura. Preparation for the "Gentleman Caller" has begun.

10. Tom has a protective concern for Laura. Their tender relationship is revealed as Tom kneels to pick up the broken pieces of glass.

11. Amanda is aware that Tom is feeling the same pressures as those felt by her husband before his desertion of her.

12. There is a strong bond of sincere love between Tom and Amanda. The tragedy is their lack of understanding for each other.

13. By cautioning Amanda, Tom indicates that something harmful could happen to Laura from Amanda's actions.

THE GLASS MENAGERIE

TEXTUAL ANALYSIS

PART 2

ACT II: SCENE 7

The scene opens with Tom, as the narrator, leaning against the grill on the fire escape landing, smoking. The music in the background creates the feeling that we have never once left Tom and the story he has been telling: The dramatic scenes have taken place only in the minds and the imaginations of the people in the audience. The atmosphere of a "memory play" persists. This mood is important to the **theme** because soon, stark reality will impose itself upon the existence of the Wingfield family and create chaos.

More About the Caller

Tom gives the audience more details about the expected "gentleman caller," Jim O'Connor. He attended the same high school as Tom and Laura. In high school, Jim walked "in a continual spotlight"; he was a star in athletics, leader of the debating team, president of the senior class, and sang the male lead in the annual light opera. He was a person of great energy and personal attraction, and very much admired by the students. He was the type that would be voted "most likely to succeed." Upon graduation, however, Jim walked out of the world in which he was so confident and into a world of adult competition. He did not succeed as rapidly as he had hoped.

Ironically, Jim and Tom find themselves in a similar position in life, and each is dependent upon the other. Jim finds satisfaction in Tom as a reminder of "his former glory"; Tom finds Jim a patient and tolerant companion because of their previous association. While the other workers at the warehouse are disdainful of Tom's interest in writing poetry, Jim regards him with humor and understanding and calls him "Shakespeare." In the narration, Tom recalls that Laura knew Jim in high-school, but he did not know to what extent their relationship grew. In any case, Jim was unaware that Laura was Tom's sister.

Amanda's Preparations

The scene shifts to the living room of the apartment. Amanda is sitting on a small table, sewing the hem of Laura's dress. The room is changed. Amanda's preparations for the gentleman caller have resulted in a new floor lamp, new covers for the chair and sofa, and a pair of new sofa pillows. Amanda is going about her chores of preparation with the meticulous care of a creative artist. Laura, too, has changed. She is standing in the middle of the room in a new dress of delicate colors, her hair looks softer and more becoming. Her whole appearance is one "of translucent glass touched by light." But Laura is nervous. She is conscious of the fact that preparations are being made for an event far more important than an evening dinner with a young man. When Amanda appears before Laura in the gown she intends to wear for the evening, with a bunch of jonquils in her arms, it becomes apparent that she is reliving her own youth and courtship with the hope that something far more successful will come of it.

The Caller Arrives

A clap of thunder is heard and Amanda shows concern over Tom and "Mr. O'Connor." When Laura hears the name of the young man coming to call, she realizes it is Jim O'Connor, the young man she has secretly admired since high school. Laura becomes upset and tells her mother that she will be unable to sit at the table with him. Amanda is adamant and insists that Laura will sit at the table and, what is more, will answer the door when they arrive.

The door bell rings. Laura is panicky, but Amanda forces her to the door and then retreats into the kitchen. As the door is opened, Laura becomes numb with fright at the sight of Jim O'Connor, but Jim does not recognize Laura as Tom introduces them. Laura, however, weakens and runs out of the room. Tom excuses Laura's behavior, telling Jim that she is shy. Embarrassed, Tom walks out onto the fire escape landing for a smoke.

Jim joins him and they start talking about their job at the warehouse. Jim observes that Tom has not been doing well in his job and that Mr. Mendoza, their boss, has also become aware of it. Tom tells Jim that his plans for the future do not include Mr. Mendoza or the warehouse, for he has decided to make a change. To fulfill his desire for adventure, he has joined the

Union of Merchant Seamen; his first month's dues were paid with the money intended for the electric light bill.

Amanda's Entrance

Amanda's voice interrupts their conversation and as they return to the living room they are met with the image of Amanda dressed in the memory of Blue Mountain; delightful, gay, and charming. Tom is surprised at his mother's appearance. Amanda looks very attractive in her dress of delicate lace and frills, and very girlish.

Comment

Tom is embarrassed, not by the way his mother looks, but because of the obvious attempt on the part of Amanda to consider Jim as her gentleman caller and not Laura's. Amanda has dressed as she would have been many years ago, when she expected a young man to call at her home in Blue Mountain.

Jim is also startled by Amanda, but her vivacity and charm win him over and he reacts very warmly. Amanda continues to entertain Jim as Tom leaves with the excuse of helping Laura prepare the dinner. While alone with Jim, Amanda attempts to impress him with the virtues of Laura. Eventually, however, the conversation is directed toward life on the Mississippi Delta. Amanda tells of herself as a pretty young Southern belle, besieged by offers from the sons of plantation owners.

Laura Becomes Ill

Tom returns and announces that dinner is on the table. As each one takes his place at the table, Amanda calls for Laura. Tom tells her Laura is not feeling well and thinks maybe she had better not join them for dinner. Amanda, graciously, but firmly, orders Laura to come to the table. As Laura appears, she becomes ill. Amanda realizes that Laura is unable to go through with it and asks Tom to help her to the sofa. He then returns to the dining room area and takes his seat. Amanda startles Tom by asking him to say a prayer before eating, a habit which has long since been forgotten in the Wingfield family. As the lights dim we see the pathetic figure of Laura, lying on the sofa, silhouetted against the background of a scene made even more awkward by the presence of an emissary from another world.

ACT II: SCENE 8

Half an hour has passed, and Amanda, Tom, and Jim are just finishing their dinner. Amanda, showing signs of having enjoyed herself, proposes a toast of dandelion wine to "the old South." Suddenly the lights go out. Jim volunteers to check the fuses while Amanda lights a candelabrum. He returns shortly and announces that nothing seems to be wrong. Amanda then accuses Tom of having forgotten to pay the electric bill. Inconvenienced but undaunted, Amanda punishes Tom by making him help her with the dishes. This, conveniently, allows Jim to be alone with Laura. Before leaving, Amanda hands Jim a glass of dandelion wine for Laura. Jim picks up the candelabrum and walks into the living room.

"Blue Roses" Again

Laura is found lying on the sofa. She sits up nervously as Jim enters. Jim senses Laura's uneasiness and starts talking to her with warmth and understanding. Eventually, Laura loses some of her shyness, and agrees to sit on the floor near the candelabrum placed there by Jim. The scene is surrounded with darkness; the candelabrum is the sole source of light.

Laura relaxes to the point of telling Jim she knew him in high school and was very fond of his singing. Jim then remembers Laura in choir practice, the one he called "Blue Roses." Laura was always late, and she admits it was due to the brace she wore on her crippled leg. The clumping sounded like thunder to her and Laura was conscious of this as she walked to her seat in the back row.

Jim accuses Laura of having been overly self-conscious, and says that because of this, she lacked confidence in making friends. He points out that everyone has problems, even him. When he left high school, he became disappointed in his slow advancement up the road of success, but he was not discouraged. He overcame his feeling of inferiority by taking courses in night school. He has now become interested in radio engineering and plans to go right to the top with the development of the industry. Excitedly, he describes how big business is built on knowledge, money, and power. Jim tells Laura that she must become interested in something in order to overcome her inferiority complex. Laura admits that she has an interest-her glass collection. It consists of little glass animals of all shapes and sizes that her mother calls her "glass menagerie."

Comment

Again, the opposition between the world of reality and the world of unreality becomes apparent. Laura speaks of her glass objects with as much interest and excitement as does Jim about the development of great industries. They both have a strong belief in what they are doing, but in the eyes of the world, Jim's aspirations are much more acceptable.

Laura and the Unicorn

Laura shows Jim her favorite glass animal. It is a very delicate unicorn. Jim hesitates to take it, but this time it is Laura's turn to instill confidence. She tells Jim she has complete trust in him. Jim takes the unicorn, and as he holds it up to the light of the candles, remarks how beautifully it shines. Laura's eyes are also shining, and for the first time, she realizes the joy of sharing an emotion. For the moment, she has completely forgotten her embarrassment in the presence of a stranger. Jim mentions that the unicorn is "extinct" and out of place in the modern world. Laura assures him that the unicorn doesn't seem to mind sitting on the shelf with the other horses.

Comment

Laura is well aware of the uniqueness of the unicorn in her menagerie. It is precisely because of this uniqueness that she has grown so fond of this piece of glass. She can place the unicorn in the midst of the other pieces in the menagerie and it will not be rejected by the "normal" animals. In real life, Laura feels that her deformity has set her apart from the normal world. Being accepted by others is a longing desire that achieves partial satisfaction in her world of glass.

The Unicorn Falls

As Jim and Laura stand looking at the reflection of light through the little glass animal, the music from the Paradise Dance Hall, across the alley, becomes audible. Setting the unicorn on the small table next to the sofa, Jim turns to Laura and asks her to dance. Laura has never danced in her life, but encouraged by her newly discovered confidence, she accepts. With instructions from Jim and the help of her own perseverance, Laura starts dancing: at first awkwardly, and then more gracefully, around the living room floor.

As they dance near the sofa, Jim's arm tightens around Laura's waist and he lifts her in the air for three complete turns. Laura squeals with joy. As her feet come to rest on the floor, the fullness of her dress sweeps over the table. A sound of breaking glass is heard and the music stops. Jim picks up the little glass horse and hands it to Laura. She examines it and finds the horn has broken off. Jim attempts to apologize, but Laura tells him it doesn't matter for now the unicorn "will feel less freakish and more at home with the other horses, the ones who don't have horns."

Jim looks at Laura and notices that she has changed. She is no longer the shy, frightened, little girl who met him at the door just a short time ago. He tells her that she is different from anyone he has known, "and all the nicer because of the difference." "They're a hundred times one thousand, but-you, well you're-Blue Roses." The music, the wine, the candlelight have all conspired to make a special moment. Unaware of his own impulses, Jim kisses Laura-the moment is broken; the world of reality and the world of unreality collide.

A Unicorn Souvenir

The danger of the blow is felt by the more practical of the two. Jim realizes that he has overstepped his bounds. He awkwardly apologizes to Laura, telling her that he is not in a position to ask for her affection: he has a girlfriend named Betty with whom he has been going steady since last summer. He explains how knowing Betty has changed his whole life; the power of love has made a new man of him. Laura stands silently as Jim recounts the incident that led to his accepting Tom's invitation to dinner, not knowing that Tom had a sister. Fearful of Laura's silence, Jim asks her to say something. Laura responds by placing the broken unicorn, a piece she still cherishes, in Jim's hand. Jim wonders at her action, but Laura tells him it's "a souvenir."

At that moment, Amanda's voice is heard singing as she enters from the kitchen. She is carrying a pitcher of lemonade and glasses and is reflecting all the exuberance of a gay occasion. She is surprised at the somber mood of Jim and Laura and attempts to liven things up with some liquid refreshment. Amanda proposes a toast "to the gaiety of the occasion." After drinking the lemonade, Amanda decides to return to the kitchen. Jim stops her by announcing that he must leave. Amanda attempts to detain Jim a little while longer. Realizing that Jim will not be detained, she invites him to call again-as often as he would like.

Jim, finding himself in an embarrassing situation, confesses to Amanda that he will be unable to return because of Betty. He explains that Betty is his fiancee and that soon, they will be married. Amanda is stunned. Jim senses the awkwardness of the situation and bids a hasty, but gracious, goodbye.

Amanda summons the remains of her Southern hospitality and wishes Jim happiness and good fortune. On his way out the door, Jim pauses to look at Laura. Her face shows no hatred or regret, just soft complacency. Jim thanks her again for the souvenir and exhorts her to remember his advice. Laura answers with a gentle smile. The gentleman caller departs.

Tom's Escape

Amanda reacts violently. All the emotion pent-up during her careful preparation and planning is released in a storm of recrimination. Tom again becomes the victim. She berates him for not knowing that his best friend is to be married-for living in a world of dreams and illusions, thinking only of his own selfish pleasures.

Tom's patience has come to an end. He feels the strong desire to extricate himself from a situation he has too long endured. Mechanically, as though it were a prearranged plan, he heads for the door. Amanda, conscious of the symptoms of a need to escape, demands to know where Tom is going. "To the movies," is Tom's reply. The fear of being deserted a second time still does not prevent Amanda from hurling a final curse at her departing son: "Go, then! Then go to the movies-you selfish dreamer!"

The lights in the living room seem to darken, until once again we are aware of the candelabrum as the sole source of illumination. Amanda crosses to Laura, who is sitting on the end of the sofa. In a scene which appears to take place behind a soundproof glass, Amanda is seen comforting Laura: the battle is over, and the war with reality is lost. Amanda stands with the tragic dignity of a vanquished leader. She is comforting Laura with gestures that are slow and graceful, almost dance-like.

Curtain

Tom re-enters and stands in a pool of light near the fire escape. He is dressed as the narrator, in the seaman's jacket and cap. Tom tells the audience that he left St. Louis and travelled around from city to city. He never stayed long in any one place, for he felt something pursuing him. Sometimes it would be a familiar bit of music, or the shape of a piece of transparent glass. It was always something that reminded him of Laura. He tried to forget her, but her image was burned indelibly on his mind. He now pleads for Laura's help; he asks her to blow out the flickering light of memory: "Blow out your candles, Laura!" As though she had heard the plea, Laura rises from the sofa, and kneeling on the floor, blows out the candles.

SUMMARY

In Act II, we realize the following points:

1. Laura resists any further adventure in the world of reality by refusing to meet Jim O'Connor.

2. Tom has made definite preparation for his means of escape by joining the Union of Merchant Seamen.

3. Jim O'Connor's adaptability to life is sharply contrasted to the adaptability of the Wingfield family.

4. Laura is capable of adjusting to the realities of life with the help of love and understanding.

5. Laura displays a strong identity with her favorite glass figure, the unicorn.

6. Jim is trying to overcome his own doubts and fears of the future by building Laura's confidence. In kissing Laura he exceeds the goal he intended. This action shows his inability to adjust his own life.

7. The Wingfields are a defeated team in the game of life, but they are persistent and will most likely continue their struggle for survival.

THE GLASS MENAGERIE

CHARACTER ANALYSES

Amanda Wingfield

The mother in Williams' play is a portrayal of his mother in real life. But she has become one of the playwright's most interesting characters solely because she was created with depth and understanding. The conflict in her life evokes feelings of sympathy and anger, and when the smoke of battle clears, an heroic nature emerges.

A Southern Gentlewoman

Williams' first achievement lay in his delineation of Southern gentlewomen. He was particularly effective in his treatment of battered characters who try to retain shreds of their former respectability. Amanda comes from a background of Southern gentility, gracious living, memories of wealthy gentleman callers, and a loving family. In the present, she has experienced nothing but challenge, hardship, and disappointment. The only balancing force between the past and the present is her family, who give her little satisfaction. Although worried about her son, whom she does not understand, and who she feels must gather himself together and face his responsibilities, Amanda is much more concerned with her daughter who, she realizes, is helpless and lost. Since her husband deserted her, the only way Amanda has been able to live with her ugly reality is to retreat into her memories. Her clothes, her speech, and her ideals for her children make her appear to be a middle-aged Southern belle, garrulous and silly, narrow and spinsterish in her attitudes toward life. At times she appears foolish and ignorant, and her approach to life seems unrealistic.

Amanda and Laura

Nevertheless, her plans for her children and her understanding of their shortcomings are realistic. She refuses to admit Laura's shyness and her crippled leg and forces her to meet young men. When Laura fails in her attempts to marry, Amanda strives to find her a place in the business world, where Laura may learn a means of self-support. Although she refuses to allow Laura to call herself a cripple and insists that her daughter consider her leg as a little physical defect that can be readily overcome by developing charm and vivacity, she is well aware of the futility of the situation.

Amanda and Tom

Her son is more difficult for her to understand because she feels that he refuses to see or accept the necessities of their life. This fact confuses Amanda, but she does not try to ignore it. She knows that her family must be held together at all costs, it is the only thing she has left. Amanda, though at times proud of her son, is insensitive to his position. She continually badgers him about his eating habits, his reading material, his smoking, his going to the movies, his late hours, and his drinking. The continual friction between Tom and his mother shows her lack of understanding. Almost every encounter leads to a quarrel.

For whatever Amanda is or does, she possesses a fighting spirit and a stubborn gallantry in the face of overwhelming odds.

She becomes domineering and masculine in insisting that Tom face the responsibility of family support, and that his need for adventure can be satisfied in his warehouse job-or that he can do without adventure. She becomes charming and feminine in her recollections of "gentleman callers" and jonquils.

"Dignity and Tragic Beauty"

But when the time for decision arrives and she must choose between failure and defeat or dignity and honor, she answers with the command, "Then go-go to the moon."

Here we see the quality that Williams suggests from the beginning as the key to her character, her heroism. At the end of the play, when Tom has left, Amanda bends over Laura, huddled upon the sofa, to comfort her. By then, the audience realizes that Amanda herself is in greater need of sympathy than the quietly resigned Laura. "Her silliness is gone and she has dignity and tragic beauty," says Williams.

Tom Wingfield

There is a weakness in the character of Tom Wingfield which is understandable only in the light of the knowledge that

Tennessee Williams was portraying himself as a young man. The final action of a son leaving his mother and crippled sister destitute in a world of hardship and despair can only be partially justified in a sympathetic understanding of a need for artistic freedom. Tennessee Williams made his escape from the trap of his suffocating family environment, but in later years, he was capable of aiding in the support of his family. Tom Wingfield's escape appears fruitless, with no indication that the future will bring satisfaction to the Wingfield family. Can Tom Wingfield's action be justified within the play?

Tom's Predicament

Tom is a sensitive young poet who is unhappy in his warehouse job and, as yet, frustrated in his poetry. He finds no satisfaction in his home life: on the contrary, he feels unmercifully committed to the support of a family that is not of his making. He feels genuine love for his mother and sister, but he is not responsible for the life they have made for themselves. He demands the right to look at life in his own terms, and eventually to meet life under those terms. He is fearfully aware that soon he must make his bid for freedom or be everlastingly trapped by two women and his own indolence. He is also aware of the suffering it will cause, and therefore must wait for a more propitious moment.

From the beginning of the play to the point of Tom's departure, we see the building of this moment. Tennessee Williams teases us, effectively, when Tom makes an emphatic exit, denouncing his mother as "an ugly babbling old witch." He returns, however, and at the insistence of Laura, apologizes for his misbehavior.

The **episode** does not go by without showing its effects on Tom. He has buffered his anguish with the narcotic effect of movies and drinking. Tom cannot leave at this time, for although the bond between mother and son is strained to the point of breaking, the bond between brother and sister has strengthened with their mutual need. However, in the last scene, after the departure of the gentleman caller, Tom's self-recrimination is not caused by Amanda, but his sorrow for Laura. He feels that through his act of inviting Jim O'Connor to dinner he has embarrassed and hurt his sister: to him, the bond of faith between brother and sister is broken. But Amanda's unjust accusations of selfishness and deceit are the propelling force that releases Tom from any further commitment to his family.

Tom "Justified"?

When Tom leaves, he escapes from a trap, a situation which is plainly unendurable, but there is nothing heroic or even positive or challenging in his departure. He has failed in his job at the shoe factory, and thereby failed in his responsibility to his family. His escape can be viewed as the action of an uncalculating, unrealistic coward. Has Williams "justified" the action of Tom? He has, in the everlasting torment of the memory of Laura. For had Tom paused for one rational moment before dismissing his responsibilities he might have noticed the look of content and satisfaction on Laura's face. Her experience with Jim had affected her, yes, but the effect was the beginning of a delayed maturity. Had her brother remained to nurture that growth, a beauty greater than anything he encountered might have been the result.

Laura Wingfield

Laura is the most pivotal character in the play: it is around her that the play revolves; it is upon her that the play depends. She is of critical importance, and yet the most passive character in the drama. Williams has created her in the image of his sister Rose. But Rose in fiction is different from Rose in real life. Williams' fondness for his sister is evident in portraying Laura as an idol of beauty, delicacy, and purity. He builds her within a protective coating of glass, and warns the world to stay away lest she become contaminated by its ills.

A Pattern of Disability

Finding it too difficult to deal with Rose's mental disability, he creates Laura with a limp and an inferiority complex to account, at least in part, for her extreme introversion. But Laura must become a real character in order to truly affect the drama. Williams makes this concession by allowing Laura to react to frustration: because of an early affliction, Laura is compelled to wear a brace; this brace causes her to retreat from the association of her classmates in school. She recalls this in terms of the horrible thumping sound it makes as she walks through the halls or as she takes her place in the back row of the choir. Eventually it leads to her dropping out of school and becoming enmeshed in a home life that is just as unsettling. Amanda's insistence that Laura prepare herself for the harsh reality of the future by enrolling in a business school ends in a further retreat from the world around her. Laura seeks an escape.

Laura's Escape

Incapable of an escape into alcohol or literature, she retreats into a world of fantasy and memory. She occupies herself with caring for tiny glass animals that are as delicate and fragile as she; she plays old phonograph records that have long since lost their connection with present reality. In her timid seclusion, Laura becomes an object of sympathy. She is reflected against the friction between Tom and Amanda as one who must be cared for, loved, and understood. When understanding comes in the form of the gentleman caller she reacts favorably. She becomes capable, for the moment, of enduring the effects of reality, because someone from the outside has shown an interest in her world. The two worlds meet, join, and become one, each capable of experiencing the effects of the other. When the gentleman caller departs, Laura is left with a taste of reality. Not completely understanding what it is that has affected her, she turns to her family for help. Again she is caught in the abyss of a family conflict. As Tom leaves, so does her only hope for survival. Laura's character, as well as her hopes, is never completely realized, and therefore remains puzzling to the audience.

Jim O'Connor

A "Realistic Character"

Williams uses the character of Jim O'Connor as a contrast to the unrealistic world of the Wingfield family. He is "an emissary from a world of reality that we were somehow set apart from," says Tom in his opening speech to the audience. He might have added "toward which we strive but can never quite attain," but he continues vaguely "he is the long-delayed, but always expected something that we live for." Whether they "live" in anticipation of fear or happiness is not explained by Tom Wingfield. Therefore, the audience must live in anticipation of the arrival of the gentleman caller. His entrance in the second act proves confusing to Tom, to Amanda, and to Laura, as well as to the audience. Confusion reigns because of an indication that Jim "is the most unrealistic character in the play." Those who believe that a realistic approach to life is the panacea for all ills are badly shaken upon the exit of Jim O'Connor.

Jim and Tom

After the initial shock of Jim's arrival is tion of the answer to all her prayers. He is the gentleman caller who exceeds all her expectations. He has a good job that pays a decent salary, and he is preparing for a career that will give him a place in the industrial development of the future. In addition, he has charm, looks, and an understanding of the art of conversation. Amanda is convinced, beyond doubt, that Laura would be content and satisfied with such a man for a husband. He symbolizes those sons of plantation owners who, many years ago, were refused the hand of a vivacious, charming, petite Southern belle; this time, he will not be refused.

Jim and Amanda

For Amanda, Jim is the personification absorbed by the Wingfield family, everything seems to progress smoothly. Tom shows his satisfaction in Jim's presence by taking him into his confidence in the scene on the fire escape. Telling Jim of his need for adventure and revealing his act of membership in The

Union of Merchant Seamen relieves Tom of some of his pent-up emotion. When they return to the apartment and Tom is confronted with the embarrassment of the "charm" of Amanda's Southern reincarnation, he is again relieved by Jim's simple, good nature. The dinner is a "success" because of the presence of someone who can easily carry on a bantering discussion with Mrs. Wingfield. When the lights go off involuntarily, it is Jim who offers to set things right, even to the point of excusing Tom's negligence in paying the light bill.

Jim and Laura

For Laura, the planned evening begins in panic, because the dream that she dared to dream has come true. For many years she has treasured a secret admiration for a high school hero. The memory of this boy has been as important to her private world as her menagerie of glass. Afraid that her imaginary world will be shattered, she refuses to risk the responsibility of meeting Jim. Soon Laura is attracted by the warmth and confidence of the young man. Their common experiences in the school choir and the memory of the incident about "Blue Roses" make it easy for Laura to forget her self-consciousness. She enjoys Jim tremendously when he talks about himself and his ambitions for the future. She is unconcerned about the lack of progress Jim has made since highschool, for in her life she can make no true evaluation of such things. She is only slightly embarrassed when he makes reference to her crippled leg and suggests that it is the cause of her sense of inferiority and her shyness in the presence of other people. When, to substantiate with authority all the things he has been telling her, he asks her to dance. Laura hesitantly agrees.

Jim's Undoing

As he takes her in his arms, "a fragile, unearthly prettiness has come out in Laura: she is like a piece of translucent glass touched by light." As Jim lifts her high in the air in their turns around the floor, Laura feels released from her little world of make-believe. When the glass unicorn falls and is broken, what to Jim seems a tragedy, is to Laura a newly discovered life for a horse that will "fell less freakish." Laura no longer needs assurance that she is a part of this new life, but Jim, driven by his own desire, kisses her. Laura regards this as an extra benefit, one that she dared not hope for, but Jim realizes that it is his undoing. He has committed himself beyond the point of propriety; he has allowed himself to run into error because of overconfidence. This fault shatters his feeling of self-assurance and he retreats back into the world of reality by awkwardly confessing his inability to love Laura as would be expected from his actions.

Consequences

Laura is gravely affected, but is willing to compromise with a token of friendship. The act of giving Jim the broken unicorn, a piece of her world, shows maturity that is not seen in the reaction of the other members of the Wingfield family. When Amanda realizes that all of her plans and hopes for the future are ruined by an emissary from the world of reality, she reacts vehemently. Her confusion causes the destruction of the only thing she has left, her family. Tom, who from Jim's arrival, has felt guilty in subjecting Laura to such an ordeal, reacts in a similar fashion. Unaware of the possible benefit derived from Jim and Laura's meeting, he relinquishes all responsibility and runs blindly for the door.

Jim cannot be blamed for being a fallible human being from the world of reality, where mistakes are possible. (But if one does not believe in a world of unreality and faces disappointment in the real world, where does the answer lie?)

The Father

The effect of the father's picture hanging in the center of the stage is that he appears as a chief character in the drama. His influence is felt from the moment the picture is first illuminated by a special spotlight, to the final scene when Tom follows in his footsteps. It is appropriate that the picture is an enlarged portrait of the likeness of Tom dressed in the uniform of the first World War.

Tom speaks of his father with a cynical reverence: "He was a telephone man who fell in love with long distance; he gave up his job with the telephone company and skipped the light fantastic out of town." He realizes that his father deserted his family and the bulk of the suffering fell on him, but he can't help but admire his father's adventurous spirit: "The last we heard from him was a picture postcard from Mazatlan, on the Pacific coast of Mexico, containing a message of two words-"Hello-Good-bye" and no address."

Tom and his Father

To Tom, his father's picture represents escape. It hangs in front of him like a prize to be won. The more he becomes like his father, the closer he is to freedom. This transformation is subtle, but constant throughout the play. It is apparent when we see Tom returning home late at night, drunk. He lies down on his bed and wonders at the feat of escaping from a coffin "without removing one nail." The image that is left in the minds of the audience at the end of the first act is the portrait of the smiling face of his father. In the second act, while expressing a need for adventure, Tom very deliberately says, "I'm like my father. The bastard son of a bastard!" It is no surprise, not even to Amanda, that Tom continues to follow a pattern of escape even to its very end.

The Father and Amanda

To Amanda, the picture recalls memories that are both bitter and sweet. Though hurt by his desertion, Amanda considers her husband the embodiment of romance. His picture stimulates thoughts of bygone days on the Mississippi Delta, of gentleman callers and jonquils. She is no longer disturbed by his memory, because years of absence have preserved only her romantic image of him. Ironically, he returns in the son to desert her for a second time.

THE GLASS MENAGERIE

CRITICAL COMMENTARY

Structure of the Play

"Memory Play"

In the production notes that always precede the text of the printed play, Williams tells us that *The Glass Menagerie* is a "memory play." This is not only in reference to a **convention** used in the play, but it can also be interpreted as a confession of the playwright. *The Glass Menagerie* follows closely the events and people in Williams' true life: experiences in St. Louis between the years of 1934 and 1936. His mother, his sister, his job in the shoe factory, and the glass menagerie were all part of his earlier life.

However, had *The Glass Menagerie* been written during his earlier years, rather than in the period between 1942 and 1944, it would have been a different play. The anger, violence, and frustration experienced by a young, sensitive playwright would surely have changed the delicate nature of the drama. But the years of separation have allowed the author an objective view of a slice of his own life: "action is softened by this patina of time and distance." Therefore, the use of the narrator to establish the play on two levels is readily understood. We see the world of reality encompassing a world of imagination to give it unity, meaning, and conflict.

The Narrator

The narrator first establishes a frame of reference with the real world by speaking directly to the audience. He introduces the time, the place, and the relative period in history. He reminds the audience of great social events, such as the revolution in Spain and labor disturbances in Chicago, Cleveland, and St. Louis. Then, to complete his promise, he introduces the characters who will give "truth in the pleasant disguise of illusion." To complete his orientation, he warns the audience, as does Williams in his preface, that they must not be disturbed by the absence of convention, because in the world of illusion any means may be employed to arrive at basic truth, and truth is sometimes destroyed by mere appearances. If the episodic nature of the drama becomes confusing, they need only to refer back to reality to find safe ground again. The narrator helps the audience in this respect by returning periodically to re-enforce the existence of the contemporary world. He alludes to familiar names and events; "Guernica," "Berchtesgaden," and "Chamberlain's umbrella."

Into the World of Memory

Having become acquainted with the context of the larger world, the audience is now guided into the world of memory. Music, composed by the noted novelist and composer, Paul Bowles, is playing in the background, because "in memory everything seems to happen to music." As they travel through the intermittent shafts of remembrance, the audience is affected by a mood of nostalgia. They see a petite, normal, middle-aged mother talking to a pale, slight, normal young daughter in what appears to be a normal nondescript apartment. The son enters and the audience recognizes him as the narrator, but he has changed. What is the reason for the change? The answer comes quickly. As all appearances dissolve, it becomes apparent that the world of illusion is a world of heartbreak, struggle, despair, and destruction, the world of illusion is one that people will make for themselves. It is the inevitable outcome of disappointment with reality. The way is clear for anyone who wishes to enter, but once you become a part of its unrealistic existence it is impossible to escape.

Against the Inevitable

Amanda Wingfield fought this inevitability, but the harder she fought the closer she came to destruction. Her husband had deserted her and she was left with the care of a crippled daughter and a son whose poetic nature rebelled against his very existence. In an attempt to save what was left of her family, Amanda alienated her son by trying to force him into a position of responsibility. Her daughter was irrevocably harmed by an exposure to a business career unsuited to her talents. When all else failed, Amanda deliberately plotted to find Laura a husband, creating a situation that ended in disaster. But the fault was not really Amanda's; she tried desperately to hold on to the present, but it kept crumbling beneath her fingers. She was trapped, as were Laura and Tom, by an existence which offered no possibility of self-fulfillment.

Tom's Plight

Tom's plight was similar to that of his mother, only his motives were not as altruistic. His job in the shoe factory offered him no satisfaction in his pursuit of self-preservation. The inner pressure created by the patience with which he endured his mother's nagging would soon lead to violence. He was forced into the decision to abandon his family. But once out in the world of reality, he realized a greater obligation to them. If the bond between him and his mother and sister had frayed, it had nevertheless held and would hold all his life.

The third member of the Wingfield family looked for no escape into the world of reality. Laura accepted her limitations and was not only willing but eager to play her passive role. She found, as did Amanda and Tom, that the world outside the Wingfield apartment was also a world of illusions, even more deceptive and destructive than the dream that held the family.

Laura's Retreat

Frustration caused by a need for escape propelled them into a world shaped by their own design: a world that became individual and personal in their quest for self-preservation. Laura's need was the greatest, and therefore her retreat into unreality showed the gravest affects. She was spared the anxiety of her search by her willingness to accept her lost state. Out of her own tender and gentle nature, she created a world of glass animals that was as delicate and fragile as she. She was their prime mover, the determining factor in their care and disposition. She was safe in the presence of her glass menagerie, and the outside world could not affect her. As each day passed, she became less inclined for adventure.

When Jim O'Connor came into her life, she reluctantly tried one more time. The effects of that misadventure caused her to return to the security of her own private world.

Tom's Escape

Unlike Laura, Tom was painfully aware of his need for escape, but his tragedy was in mistaking illusion for reality. He escaped from the drudgery of a monotonous job by writing poetry in the washroom and on the tops of shoe boxes. This activity resulted in his dismissal from his employment and the loss of support for his family. He escaped from the anguish he felt in the presence of his mother by spending nights in the movies and bars and daydreaming about romantic adventures. When he finally found himself in the midst of the darkness of these adventures, he discovered that he was not conditioned for a life of reality, and he became possessed with the guilt of leaving reality behind in the form of a struggling mother and a pathetic sister.

Amanda's Illusion

Amanda was the only character who found that she could successfully cover the wounds of reality with the salve of illusion. The memories of Blue Mountain, when she was a desirable young Southern aristocrat with an abundance of gentleman callers at her feet, protected her from the harsh realities of life. The fond remembrance of her husband as a symbol of a romantic youth filled with parties, dances, picnics, and jonquils have numbed the pain of his desertion. Obviously, Amanda was aware of the sacrifice necessary to keep her small family together. She tried to prepare Tom for this sacrifice by telling him "the world is full of young men employed in warehouses and offices and factories" who find "adventure in their careers." She tried to forewarn him of the fact that "the future becomes the present, the present the past, and the past turns into everlasting regret if you don't plan for it." She does not ignore these facts, and spirited by her memories, she was willing to accept the struggle.

The World and The Wingfields

But the struggle of the Wingfields becomes less significant when we compare it to the struggle of the society of the ailing and torn outside world. The depression had left its mark on a world that had barely survived the shock of a resounding World War. Possessed by a feeling of fear and uncertainty and deceived by the appearance of a rising economy, all of society was experiencing the pleasures of a weekend drunk. Meanwhile, underneath this calm but shakey exterior fermented the ingredients for a second World War. Society reveled in the illusions created by hot swing music and liquor, dance halls, bars, movies and sex, afraid to face the realities of world conflict. But the outcome was inevitable, and many people found themselves in the same trap as the Wingfields, forced to cope with a situation for which they were not equipped. So the Wingfields' struggle for survival, though minor by comparison, was indicative of the ills of a nation.

Williams' Production Techniques

A commentary on any of Williams' plays is incomplete without a reference to his use of production techniques: his stage settings, use of lights, and music. Williams has been fortunate in working with very talented people. However, his great knowledge and experience in the theater have made him sensitive of the impact gained through the use of all aspects of the medium.

Projected Images and Legends

In his production notes for *The Glass Menagerie,* Williams originally suggested the use of a screen for visual images. This unconventional technique was suggested as a means of creating a greater unity throughout the play. Being fearful of the possibility that the audience would become confused by the episodic nature of the drama, he wished to have pictures and legends flashed on a screen simultaneously with the action of the play. His intention was to add a greater significance to the meaning of what was being said. For example, in the scene between Jim and Laura while the reference to "Blue Roses" is being discussed, the legend on the screen points out the peculiarity of the name, and the audience, along with Laura, is made more keenly aware that although blue is beautiful, it is wrong for roses.

Other uses of this same device were not as effective. In the scene in which Amanda talks about her seventeen gentleman callers, the legend to be flashed on the screen is a French rendition of Francois Villon's famous tribute to beautiful women. Or, during the scene in which Amanda is warning Laura of the possibility of her becoming a dependent old maid, this lovely speech is distracted by a legend about the crust of humility, an incongruous intrusion. Thirty-nine uses of this device were included in the original script.

Although he agreed that the idea of the screen images had merit, the director of the first Broadway production, Eddie Dowling, wisely decided not to use them. The magnificence of Laurette Taylor's portrayal of Amanda proved them unnecessary. Williams accepted the absence of his screen theory and admitted the effectiveness of the New York production, but he is inclined to believe that there is a great deal to be gained by their use. In fact, the possibilities of the device, says Williams, "seem much larger than the instance of this play can possibly utilize."

Stage Setting

To prove the strength of Williams theatrical convictions, one must consider the stage setting for *Menagerie*. The play is located in the heart of the St. Louis tenement district. The dark wall of the exterior of the apartment and the surrounding alley are in marked contrast to the memories of Amanda's earlier life. This contrast is constantly referred to in her insistence that all vestiges of gracious living are "gone, gone, gone." The fire escape becomes a poor excuse for a terrace, and when she places her good silverware on the dining room table, it becomes a memorable occasion. In a memory play the artist can use unusual freedom from stage **convention** as does Williams in his description of the set.

The stage is divided into two main areas: the interior of the apartment with its division of dining room and living room; and the exterior, with its fire escape and an alley with a clothesline and trash cans. Since the play shifts between memory and reality, it demands simultaneous staging for both. The set accommodates this need by means of transparent "flats." In a moment, the action can change from the exterior to the interior within full view of the audience. These transparent walls also create an aesthetic effect which is most appropriate to "memory." The scene in which Laura is separated from the dinner party by a mystic curtain dropped between the living room and dining room is a good example.

Location of Objects

The location of important objects within the areas is also definitely established by Williams. The father's picture, which has a significant role in the play, must hang on a wall facing-and in full view of-the audience. The phonograph, used as a form of escape for Laura, is in a position where her movement toward it becomes conspicuous. Because the living room is close to the audience, the glass menagerie cannot help but be noticed. The dining room table is situated in a position that seems far removed from the audience, so that scenes played in this area give an added impression of memory.

Use of Music

This impression is augmented by the skillful use made of music by the author. The main **theme** is a tune called "The Glass Menagerie," which is primarily Laura's music and is heard most clearly when the play focuses upon her and "the lovely fragility of glass which is her image." It is music that suggests the delicate nature of spun glass that can be easily broken. It is as interminable and as distant as echoes from a circus parade. The **theme** is used as a means of unifying the drama. It keeps recurring after each episode to sustain the mood of the play.

There is also the music from the old phonograph records left to Laura by her father. When played, they convey a feeling of detachment from the world of the present. Laura plays the records when she is alone or when she feels the need to escape the scrutiny of her mother.

The music from the Paradise Dance Hall gives the audience the feeling that the outside world is trying to find its way into the apartment. As Tom stands on the fire escape listening to it, he feels a strange longing for adventure. He resists its compelling force until the anguish and torment of his home life weakens him. When Jim O'Connor opens the apartment door and lets the music flow into the room, Laura becomes a different person; she is made vulnerable to love and adventure.

Williams' Lighting

Having established his requirements for the setting and music, Williams adds his suggestions for lighting. "Being a memory play, it is dimly lighted" to depict the sentimental mood of the drama. He follows emotion with the skillful use of isolated light. During the first big quarrel between Amanda and Tom in the dining room, "the upstage area is lit with a turgid smoky red glow," while Laura, standing in the living room is contrasted in a "clear pool of light." This effect creates a definite focus on Laura's panic-stricken reaction to a major conflict within the family. The use of the flashing neon sign of the Paradise Dance Hall across the alley is a constant reminder to Tom that out there lies adventure.

Amanda is isolated in a pool of light during her memory scene or while talking on the telephone, indicating that these moments belong to her. In the final scene of the play, during the dinner with the gentleman caller, Laura is seen lying on the sofa in a light "having a peculiar pristine clarity" while the light on the dinner is dim. All of the lighting suggested by Williams adds to the expression of character, mood, and situation.

A Final Candle

His most masterly stroke comes in the play's final moment. All of the lights go out. For a moment we are left in darkness, just long enough to transcend the bleak interior of the Wingfield apartment and then into a world of candlelight: a world in which anything can happen, and does. Isolated from the grim reminder of the world in which she lives, Laura finds new strength, new possibilities, and new adventure. When failure and disappointment come at the end of the play, the audience is no longer reminded of a chair, a sofa, or a dining room table, but of the struggle of people with one flickering hope which can be snuffed out like the light of a candle.

SUMMARY

In *The Glass Menagerie* it is evident that Tennessee Williams has found a dramatic technique suitable to his talents. He started his writing career by writing poetry, an individual, personal, subjective art. Because, of his involvement in the theater, Williams moved out of the realm of esoteric art and began writing plays for large audiences. In *Menagerie*, the delicate, sympathetic, and sensitive nature of a poet is mixed with the objective creation of meaningful people in a meaningful situation. His use of the exchange shifts of scene between reality and memory could have presented many problems, had he not possessed the talent capable of establishing such a form. Williams' knowledge of visual and musical effects, coupled with a genius for dialogue, have made *The Glass Menagerie* his most effective poetic work.

THE GLASS MENAGERIE

ESSAY QUESTIONS AND ANSWERS

Question: Discuss some of the major **themes** expressed in *The Glass Menagerie.*

Answer: One of Tennessee Williams favorite **themes** concerns the attempt of women who have been defeated in life to reclaim some shreds of respectability. Blanche Du Bois, in *A Streetcar Named Desire*, is an excellent example of this **theme**. We also see this trait in the character of Amanda. She was cradled in the lap of Southern aristocracy. Her visions of the South recall stately mansions, huge plantations, beautiful rivers and streams, and a rolling countryside full of jonquils and jasmine. She was preoccupied with gentleman callers, dances, picnics, and pink lemonade. In the rear apartment of a St. Louis tenement building, the existence of back alleys, factories, light bills and the support of a family is bleak by comparison. Amanda attempts to restore the essence of this faded culture by retaining its style of conversation, its mannerisms and appearances. Nevertheless, the gaiety, beauty, and tenderness of her girlhood no longer exists.

A recurring **theme** of loneliness is evident in this as well as in other plays of Williams. Amanda's loneliness is caused by a lack of understanding and a need for communication with her children. Her years of concern for their growth and welfare have only resulted in her alienation from them. Her difficulty in understanding why Tom is not happy in his job at the shoe factory shows that she has lost all contact with the adventurous desires of the young. Necessity has made her a lonely woman.

Because of his inability to make Amanda understand his feelings, Tom has also become lonely. Due to his sensitive nature, his loneliness is more acute. He is cursed with a poet's means of communication and his fertile imagination makes him unable to establish any worthwhile relationship with his less-endowed coworkers. Tom's loneliness increases when he realizes that the world outside the Wingfield family is no more sympathetic or understanding than the world within it.

Laura does not suffer loneliness as do Amanda and Tom. Her loneliness is natural to her, for she has never been able to communicate successfully. Because of her introverted nature, Laura has never felt a desire to associate with anyone outside the members of her family. When circumstance presented her with the opportunity to emerge from her quiet and uneventful state, she found nothing but unhappiness and a deeper loneliness. This condition, Williams seems to suggest, is one of the root conditions of humanity, and was to become one of the dominant **themes** in all the playwright's work.

The main **theme** of *The Glass Menagerie* is the need for understanding, tenderness, and fortitude among individuals trapped by circumstance. The play presents the audience with characters and a situation that are genuine. Despite their moodiness and foolishness and self-deception, the destruction of their dreams and aspirations is significant. From the beginning it is apparent that everyone in the play is a failure, and as the play progresses it becomes clear that they are also doomed to a life of suffering.

Williams tells us that the sins of the world lie in the attempts of people to cover up their inefficiencies. People realize their shortcomings, but rather than admit them, they attempt to cover them with the mask of illusion. The result of such deception is destruction; either in war between nations, between two people, or within the individual. This does not always mean total destruction, however, for some people find a strange satisfaction in suffering; it almost as though they were atoning for their sins.

Not one of the characters in *Menagerie* can cope with his situation. They all, with the exception of Laura, make a brave attempt, but because of their inadequacies, they fail. It is not their fault: they are just too helpless to do more than delay the inevitable. Therefore, they revert to the mask of illusion: Amanda to the memories of childhood; Tom to the movies and the bars; and Laura to the glass menagerie. They were all doomed from the beginning, and for a time, their struggles will allow them to survive, but they will never triumph. The beauty and magic of *The Glass Menagerie* is that this pathos is genuine and deeply moving.

Question: To Tennessee Williams, symbols are an important means of poetic expression. Discuss some of the major symbols used in *The Glass Menagerie.*

Answer: The glass menagerie is the most obvious symbol in the play. Its great significance is in terms of Laura. She created the menagerie out of a need to escape from a world full of frustration in the form of social obligations, business schools, and her surrounding living conditions. In the world of little glass animals, Laura sees beauty, delicacy, and a cold impersonality. They are all features which she admires and with which she can live. She maintains the menagerie to suit her own design. She is the prime mover, the determining factor in the disposition of all the animals. Therefore she is depended upon and has the feeling of being needed. To Laura, the glass menagerie is not a world of illusion, but a real world. When she comes in contact with it, the cold glass becomes warm, heated by the warmth of her own body. This warmth breathes life into the glass creatures, and when she is there, it is a living world. She can control the inducing factor of life. In the world outside the menagerie, Laura is subject to the whims of fate, but even there she feels supported by her confidence in her illusive power. When she loses that confidence, she becomes nothing and therefore no longer exists. Laura does exist because of the glass menagerie.

Blue Mountain is a symbol of escape for Amanda Wingfield. It is a means by which she can rid herself, momentarily, of her present miserable circumstances. Like Laura, she too has her glass menagerie, but her collection is one of memories that glow brighter with the passing years. She doesn't get lost in her illusions, like Laura, because it is not a world that she creates, but rather adventures that she relives. She had once felt the fulfillment of the experience of entertaining seventeen gentleman callers in one day, of attending grand balls surrounded by the scent of magnolias and the color of jonquils. She is not caught up in the process of giving new life to her dreams. She is satisfied in the reminiscence of a life that had once been lived to its fullest, but now is past never to be lived the same way again. Amanda depends upon these memories, however, and could not face life without them. They refresh her and sustain her because they remind her that once in her life there was beauty and gentility.

The symbol of the Paradise Dance Hall is adventure for Tom Wingfield with all of its characteristics: flashing lights, music, and people having a wonderful time. It adds to the other symbols of escape for Tom, such as the movies, the bars, and the writing of poetry, but the name, Paradise, has even a greater significance, because it affects not only Tom, but the outside world. It is a symbol of cynicism. Paradise means pleasure but in this instance it is just momentary pleasure. People can come and for a few short hours forget the pain that brought them there. It is an escape from the effects of the Depression, the war which is rapidly enveloping the world, and the failures encountered in everyday life. Everyone looks for his own Paradise Dance Hall in one form or another.

As the play begins, one of the first things the audience notices is the weird lattice-work outline of the fire escape. Williams calls it "a structure whose name is a touch of accidental poetic truth, for all those huge buildings are always burning with the slow and implacable fires of human desperation." It is on this fire escape that Tom Wingfield finds relief from the burning pressures that are kindling inside the apartment. From the fire-escape landing he can see the adventure he so desires. It is just a matter of a few steps down to freedom, but it often takes a lifetime of courage to take them. Amanda complains that the fire escape is "a poor excuse for a porch," but she finds that she can sit on it as "gracefully and demurely as if she were settling into a swing on a Mississippi veranda." Laura finds no need for the fire escape. It just becomes a hindrance to her as she goes about her daily chores of shopping for her mother. She is not capable of an escape via the fire escape. It is no mere accident, however, when Tom, the adventurer, uses it as his avenue to freedom.

Laura's choicest possession in the menagerie is the lonely and unique unicorn. She finds a close attachment to this little glass animal, because it is a symbol of herself. In the realm of the modern world, the unicorn is a freak, a fantasy, but when it is placed in the world of glass the other animals don't seem to mind a bit. The horn on its head is the identifying factor, just as a fragile young girl with a brace on her leg might be recognized by it. Both can radiate beauty and delicacy, but because they are not like the others, they must live a life of cold isolation. Break the horn, and a renewed confidence begins to glow. Show the girl with the brace that she can still dance and she begins to act like any normal young lady. When she realizes that life hasn't changed by the absence or existence of a brace, she becomes something that can be given away or disposed of like a broken piece of glass. Laura's identification with the unicorn is complete to the very end of a broken life.

The final important symbol of the play is Jim O'Connor, the gentleman caller. He is considered a symbol of reality to the Wingfield family: something that is set apart from them, but something they always desire. He comes as an answer to Amanda's hopes for the future. Laura is also moved with expectancy, but he turns out to be a disappointment. The reason become evident if Jim's character is understood.

Although he is an emissary from the real world he, too, has illusions. He must have them to cope with his own expectations, the future world of industrial development. To prevent himself from thinking about his disappointments of the past six years, he is preparing for his illusion: he is going to night school so that when industry starts going, he will go right up with it. In the meantime, he must keep up a brave and cheerful exterior, never attempting to question himself or his illusion too deeply. Jim's illusion is one that can be accepted by a realist. He is gambling on something that is not entirely of his own making. He has a chance for success.

Question: Discuss the importance of Tom Wingfield both as the narrator and as a character in the drama.

Answer: The use of Tom as a narrator presents the drama with a double focus: the world of reality and the world of illusion. One helps to complement, unify, and control the other. The narrator has greater perspective on the troubled lives of the Wingfields because he is removed in time and space. He is able to understand and appreciate the suffering endured by Amanda; he is able to understand that although she has deeply hurt him and Laura, she has done everything because she loves them deeply. But within the drama, Tom finds it difficult to tolerate his mother's lack of understanding for him. He became angry and impatient with her because he sees her as a foolish and embarrassing old woman, whose main intention in life seems to be to force him into a position of responsibility which he is not willing to accept. Because of his sensitive nature and his desire to become a writer, he feels imprisoned from the adventures of the rest of the world. He becomes confused and violently frustrated. Removed from the situation, Tom the narrator regards his mother with compassion, compassion he was never able to show her when he lived under the same roof. The play he narrates is itself a proof of his compassion. In it, his mother is not the villain, but one of four lonely people caught in a trap not of her own making.

As the narrator, Tom is also an emissary from the outside world. He sees and narrates the ills of a society in conflict. He has come to see that the Wingfield family is not the only family lost in illusions. The whole world is taking refuge in illusion-from the Depression, from the oncoming war, from the pettiness of their own private lives. As a younger man, he is essentially concerned with himself. He sees the outside world as a quest for freedom, with an atmosphere of limitless possibilities. He also makes the mistake of interpreting illusion for reality. But Tom the narrator is wiser now. He can see the sufferings of the Wingfield family as being multiplied "a thousand times one thousand." He sees and can understand the futile war that is being waged by people like himself: people who will fight for their freedom only to find that for every victory there is a price to be paid. The use of the greater world of reality surrounding and encompassing the necessary world of illusion is the unifying force in Williams' drama.

A STREETCAR NAMED DESIRE

INTRODUCTION

The evening of March 31, 1945, marked a memorable day in the annals of American Theater. The New York drama critics, along with hundreds of theater enthusiasts, witnessed the arrival of one of America's most promising young playwrights, Tennessee Williams. The opening night of *The Glass Menagerie* did not meet with the unanimous approval of the critics; the memory of a Boston failure, *Battle of Angels* in 1940, was still vividly recalled. Two years later, on December 3, 1947, the expectations of Williams' faithful admirers were undeniably justified: *A Streetcar Named Desire* opened at the Ethel Barrymore Theater in New York City. It was acclaimed as "the most moving American play of the past dozen years." Tennessee Williams' career as a playwright was fully established but not without anguish and difficulties.

CHARACTERS

Blanche DuBois-aging Southern belle; sister to Stella.

Stella Kowalski-sister of Blanche; wife of Stanley.

Stanley Kowalski-husband of Stella.

Harold (Mitch) Mitchell-friend of Stanley; suitor to Blanche.

Steve Hubbell-friend of Stanley; husband of Eunice.

Eunice Hubbell-friend of Stella; wife of Steve.

Negro Woman-friend of Stella and Eunice.

Mexican Woman-flower vendor.

Pablo Gonzalez-friend of Stanley.

Young Man-collects for newspapers.

A Doctor-takes Blanche away to the asylum.

A Nurse-accompanies the doctor.

SETTING

A slum area of New Orleans, called Elysian Fields.

TIME

The late 1940s.

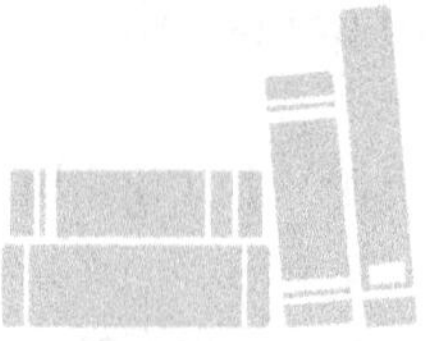

A STREETCAR NAMED DESIRE

TEXTUAL ANALYSIS

SCENES 1 - 3

SCENE ONE

The scene opens on an early evening in May. The darkening blue sky reveals the outline of a two story corner building on a street in New Orleans called Elysian Fields. A faded white staircase, on the right side of the stage, leads to the doors of two flats, one upstairs and one down. In the background, music can be heard emanating from a bar just around the corner. The tune is slow and mournful, it is played in the style of a Negro entertainer on a "blue piano." This music is heard as a **theme** throughout the play. The music adds charm to an otherwise poor and decaying environment. In the dull blue glow, that illuminates the outside stair area, we see Eunice, a white occupant of the upstairs flat, talking with a colored neighbor from down the street. Around the corner come two men, Stanley Kowalski and Harold Mitchell (Mitch). They are about twenty-eight or thirty years old, dressed in working clothes. As they stop at the foot of the stairs, Stanley calls to his wife Stella. She appears from out of the downstairs flat, mildly irritated by hearing her name hollered in the streets. Stanley throws her a package of meat which she manages to catch, protestingly. Then, with a smile, she asks Stanley if she can go bowling with him. He, already around the corner and on his way, answers "yes." Stella puts the meat away and runs off to catch her husband.

Comment

In these first few moments of the play it is apparent that Stella comes from an entirely different background than her husband. She is a young woman of about twenty-five years of age and has a gentle and graceful manner. It is obvious that her standard of living was much beyond the situation we see her in at the present time. Stanley, on the other hand, is a person who has lived, and is capable of living, a much rougher existence than his wife.

After a moment of silence, filled only with the laughter of the two women on the steps, another figure appears from around the corner. It is Blanche DuBois carrying a valise. She is dressed in a manner which is totally out of place in her present surroundings. She is daintily dressed in white with a necklace, earrings of pearl, white gloves and a hat. She appears to be about five years older than her sister Stella. Her uncertain manner indicates a delicate nature which requires protection. She is obviously disturbed by her surroundings and keeps looking nervously at a slip of paper in her hand. Eunice, finally noticing Blanche, asks her if she is lost. Much distressed, Blanche repeats the directions she was given: "To take a streetcar named Desire, and then transfer to one called Cemeteries and get off at Elysian Fields."

Comment

These directions are an obvious attempt on the part of the playwright to establish a symbolic motif for the play. They indicate that Blanche was brought to Elysian Fields by means of desire and despair, or death.

Eventually, the truth is revealed to Blanche that her sister, Mrs. Stanley Kowalski, lives in this neighborhood and in this very building, the lower flat. Eunice also tells her that Stella can be found around the corner watching her husband bowl. The Negro Woman offers to fetch her while Eunice takes Blanche into the lower flat to wait. As they enter, a dull blue light discloses the interior of the apartment. It consists of two rooms: a kitchen which contains a bed at the far end, eventually used by Blanche, and a second room, a bedroom, off which is a bathroom. Blanche is noticeably startled by the crude appearance of the flat. Eunice, aware of the fact that Blanche is Stella's sister, and that they were born and raised on a plantation in Mississippi, asks about "The great big place with white columns," Belle Reve. Blanche is very tired and finds talking with Eunice a chore she cannot endure. She indicates to Eunice that she desires to be left alone. Good-naturedly, Eunice leaves with the intention of hurrying Stella. Blanche sits in the semi-darkness for a moment without moving. She appears frightened of something more than her present situation. A cat screeches and she catches her breath with a startled gesture. Suddenly she notices something in a half opened closet. She springs up and crosses to it, and removes a whiskey bottle. She pours a half tumbler of whiskey and tosses it down. Carefully, she replaces the bottle and washes out the tumbler at the sink. Then she resumes her seat in front of the table. Stella enters on the run calling her sister's name. She stops when she sees Blanche and for a moment they stare at each other. Then they come together in a frantic embrace. In a moment of hysterical comment, Blanche blurts out her feelings about Stella being found in such a horrible place. Blanche then expresses a need for a drink of liquor to calm her nerves. As Stella pours Blanche a drink, a look of nervous relief comes over Blanche's face.

Comment

It is rather incongruous that Blanche, who presents herself as an example of good manners and gentle living, should find such great need for liquor.

Blanche now continues to criticize Stella's way of life in New Orleans. Stella doesn't seem to be at all disturbed by her own existence so Blanche decides to change the subject. Feeling committed to explain why she visited her sister unexpectedly, Blanche tells her story. While teaching in a high school, Blanche felt the need for a rest. Her superintendent suggested that she take a leave of absence before the term was officially over. While talking, it becomes obvious that Blanche is desirous of another drink of liquor, but when Stella offers to pour another Blanche refuses with the false admonition that one is her limit. As the two women continue talking. Blanche realizes that the apartment has only two rooms and she will be required to sleep in the kitchen with no door between the rooms. Stella explains that this condition is not unusual in their level of society. Blanche then becomes concerned about Stanley. In explaining Stanley's character Stella cautions Blanche not to compare him with the type of men they went out with in Mississippi. Stanley is rough and crude, but he is also handsome and lovable and she tells Blanche how much she misses him when he is away on a business trip. Blanche is amused and somewhat revolted by her sister's feelings for someone who swept her off her feet with his virility. Nevertheless, it cannot be denied that Stella is very much in love with her husband. Blanche becomes somewhat envious of her sister's happiness and begins to tell of all the hardships she has endured since Stella left Belle Reve. Blanche becomes slightly hysterical as she tells Stella of the loss of their family home. Stella is dumb-founded with disbelief. Thinking her sister is reproaching her for the loss, Blanche enumerates how Stella abandoned Belle Reve as soon as she was able and left its responsibility to her. She tells of the death and continued destruction of family and property to the point where nothing was left. First their father and mother died, then their sister Margaret, followed by their cousin Jessie. Death is expensive and Blanche was forced to sell bits and pieces of their family home to pay expenses. No one came to her aid.

Comment

Blanche feels deeply the loss of Belle Reve. It was the last remnant of a life and tradition that she greatly admired. Now gone, she attempts to cling to this dream with the use of manners, speech, and habits that are foolishly out of place.

Blanche concludes her story by admonishing Stella, for while all this was taking place she was in the arms of her "Polack" husband. Stella begins to cry and goes into the bathroom to wash her face. The sound of men's voices is heard outside. Blanche, apprehensive at meeting Stanley, darts into the bedroom. The end of a conversation about a poker game scheduled for the following evening is heard as Stanley enters. He is of medium height, about five feet eight or nine, and strongly, compactly built. Because of his animal instincts, Stanley notices Blanche immediately. For a moment they stand staring at each other, sizing each other up. Then Blanche introduces herself and Stanley responds with similar words and gestures.

Comment

They are both uneasy; Stanley, because of his crudeness which only becomes apparent to him in situations like these and Blanche, for reasons which will become apparent later. It is obvious that they are two entirely different people and that true harmony will never exist between them.

Stanley offers Blanche a drink which she refuses immediately on the grounds that she rarely touches it. Stanley then observes the depletion of his liquor by saying "some people rarely touch it, but it touches them often." Stanley next decides to take off his sweaty bowling shirt before he catches cold. Affected by his crudeness, yet admiring his manliness, Blanche becomes tired and faint. Stanley attempts to carry on this awkward conversation by recalling to mind that Blanche was once married. Blanche admits that she was married when very young and that her husband had since died. Overcome with emotions, Blanche's head falls on her arms, the music of the Varsouviana is heard in the distance as the scene ends.

SUMMARY

In this scene the following points become evident:

1. Stella and Stanley have come from different backgrounds, but they have found something in their married life that is mutually satisfying.

2. Blanche, although strong in her convictions, is physically weak and needs protection. Also, her nervous disposition comes from something other than her discontent with Stella's situation.

3. The contrast between the two sisters-Stella as the normal, happy, and average woman; Blanche as the refined, hypersensitive, and decadent aristocrat-is clear.

4. The contrast between Blanche and Stanley indicates that the arrival of this older sister will threaten the happy marital arrangement between Stella and Stanley.

SCENE TWO

It is six o'clock the following evening. The "blue piano" can be heard in the distance. It is the evening of Stanley's poker party. Stella, fearful that Blanche would find meeting Stanley's friends agonizing, has made plans to take Blanche out for the evening. Blanche is taking a bath while Stella finishes with her primping. Stanley enters from the outside and seeing Stella dressed in her best clothes questions her about her plans. He is very disturbed to hear that Stella and Blanche will be eating at Galatoire's, a very fashionable restaurant, while he is to be satisfied with a cold plate. Overcoming this irritation, he again becomes disturbed at hearing of the loss of Belle Reve. Stella pleads for Stanley's understanding and asks him to be nice to Blanche. Stanley only becomes more irritated and explains to Stella the Napoleonic Code. It is a statute in the State of Louisiana that states that any possession belonging to one or the other of a married couple belongs to both. Stanley, therefore, shows a personal interest in the loss of Stella's childhood home. He accuses Blanche of trying to swindle them. Stella professes her sister's innocence in business affairs and confesses that Blanche has no idea what happened to the money. Stanley stalks into the bedroom and throws open Blanche's wardrobe trunk which stands in the middle of the room. He shows Stella all the beautiful clothes and the jewelry Blanche owns. Being a very poor judge of such things, Stanley does not realize that all of Blanche's possessions are cheap imitations. Stella attempts to point this fact out to her stubborn husband, but he refuses to be dissuaded and an argument ensues. Angrily, Stella walks out on to the stair landing and demands that Stanley follow her to allow Blanche to dress in peace. Feeling that his manhood is being tested, Stanley refuses to budge. At that moment, Blanche emerges from the bathroom freshly bathed and scented, and feeling like a brand new human being. She utters a greeting to Stanley as she closes the drapes between the rooms. Conscious of Stanley standing on the other side of the drapes Blanche starts a meaningless conversation. She makes reference to the trunk being open and her clothes pulled out. Stanley tells her that he and Stella were helping her to unpack. Finally, Blanche asks Stanley to come and help her with the buttons on the back of her dress. Stanley crosses into the room and while he makes a clumsy attempt at the buttons, Blanche begins an innocent flirtation with him. Stanley brings this to an end by demanding to see the papers of the sale of Belle Reve. Blanche tells him they are in the trunk, whereupon Stanley tears open the trunk and begins to look through the papers he finds in it. One package, with a ribbon tied around, is a bunch of old love letters written to Blanche by her late husband. She grabs for them and in the struggle they cascade to the floor. Angry and hurt, Blanche shouts that she will now have to burn the letters because the touch of Stanley's hands "insults them." Stanley, taken back by this remark, allows Blanche to sort out the papers pertaining to Belle Reve. She hands them to him and he discovers that her story was true: Belle Reve was lost on a mortgage. Blanche then explains how her grandfathers, father, uncles, and brothers squandered the land away on their wild, irresponsible escapades. Stanley, feeling somewhat sheepish, tries to relieve his guilt by explaining the Napoleonic Code and the fact that he was looking after the interests of his wife's affairs-especially now that she is going to have a baby. Blanche is startled by this news and runs out to congratulate Stella. Stella, in turn, apologizes for her husband's behavior. Blanche, a bit shaky from the affair, but satisfied that she held her own, confesses the merit in mixing Stanley's blood with the blood of those who lost Belle Reve. The baby will be well received. Steve and Pablo appear for the poker game, carrying a case of beer. In the distance can be heard the "blue piano" and the voice of a vendor selling "red-hots."

SUMMARY

The main objective in this scene was to establish the duel for supremacy between Blanche and Stanley. Stanley is fighting for his manhood, his virility, his dominance over women; the only things he has confidence in. Blanche is fighting to establish righteous indignation in the eyes of men. The first round ended with Blanche the victor, a situation Stanley feels must be righted.

SCENE THREE

It is 2 o'clock the following morning and the poker game is still going on in the kitchen. The light from a green shaded light fixture hanging over the kitchen table illuminates the figures of four husky, young men. On the table can be seen watermelon slices, whiskey bottles, and glasses. The rest of the stage is lit from the spill of the kitchen light. For a moment there is silence while a hand is dealt, then the usual conversation as the bidding begins. It is apparent that Stanley is still feeling the effects of his encounter with Blanche; he is irritated with Mitch for wanting to go home. Mitch has a sick mother to whom he is very devoted, she waits up until he gets home at night. Just then Blanche and Stella appear from around the corner of the building. Realizing the game is still in progress, Blanche prepares herself for the inevitable meeting with Stanley's friends. As they walk into the kitchen Stella introduces Blanche to the men. Stanley shows contempt for Blanche in remarking that the men needn't stand. Stella retorts by asking Stanley to bring the game to an end. Stanley orders the women out of the room. Stella and Blanche cross into the bedroom and pull the drapes closed.

Blanche, disturbed by this last encounter, decides to take a bath to calm her nerves. As she heads for the bathroom, Mitch emerges with towel in hand. Stella introduces him to Blanche. Blanche can see that Mitch is different from the others; he is more courteous and considerate. She is pleased to hear that he is not married. As the men continue playing cards Stella and Blanche become engaged in a women's type conversation. The noise of their voices irritates Stanley and he tells them to shut up! Stella is angered by this, but realizing Stanley has been drinking, she decides not to pursue the argument. She crosses into the bathroom as Blanche turns on a little radio sitting on top of her trunk. Rhumba music is heard throughout the apartment. Stanley jumps to his feet and despite assurances from the other men that the radio is not disturbing them, he rushes in and switches it off. Angry now, Stanley picks on Mitch. He accuses him of looking through the opening in the drapes at Blanche undressing. The rest of the men kid Mitch about winning all the money. Mitch, feeling uncomfortable, reacts good-naturedly to the comments and heads for the bathroom. As he walks through the drapes he sees Blanche who tells him that "the little boys' room is busy right now." Blanche asks Mitch for a cigarette. As Mitch offers his cigarette case, Blanche remarks how beautiful it is. Mitch explains that it was a gift from a girl whom he had loved. She has since died. Blanche sympathizes with Mitch-and the bond between them is complete.

Comment

Blanche feels a need for protection. She realizes that in this jungle of degeneracy, that is now to be her home, she must find a friend. Mitch, with his decency, courtesy, and potential for understanding, might be the one. Mitch, whose mother is ill and dying, feels a need for someone to take her place; someone who will be as perfect as his mother. As yet, he has not met a girl like this; no modern girl is. Perhaps Blanche, with her obsession for tradition, is the girl.

They begin to talk rather freely. Blanche tells Mitch a little of her past, that she is a schoolteacher and that her name, DuBois, is derived from the French Huguenots. In the midst of their conversation she asks Mitch to hang a Chinese lantern, which she brought with her, over the light bulb in the room: "I can't stand a naked light bulb, anymore than I can a rude remark or a vulgar action." She finds that the flirtation lost on Stanley works very well on Mitch. As Stella comes out of the bathroom, Blanche, in order to keep Mitch's interest, asks him to dance. She turns on the radio and they commence to waltz. Stanley charges fiercely through the drapes into the bedroom. He grabs the radio and with a shouted oath, he throws it out the window. Stella curses Stanley for his drunken act and runs into the kitchen to break up the poker game. Stanley follows, grabs her, and drags her into a dark corner of the kitchen. There is the sound of a blow. Stella cries out. Blanche screams and runs into the kitchen. The men rush forward and there is grappling and cursing. Something is overturned with a crash. Stanley is finally forced into the bedroom by the two men. Stella runs out the door crying. With a strange satisfaction, Blanche runs into the bedroom and demands Stella's clothes. She gathers up some things from a closet. Then goes outside where Stella is waiting and helps her up the stairs to Eunice's flat.

Comment

The fierce fight between Stella and Stanley gives Blanche great satisfaction. From the moment she entered the Kowalski household she has been trying to weaken Stella's strong love for her husband. At last she has been successful.

Stanley stands dazed like a losing prize fighter. The men rush him into the bathroom and under the shower. Sounds of curses and shouts are heard amid the splashing of water. Suddenly the men run for the poker table and sweep up their winnings on their way out. The door closes on them and the place is still. The Negro entertainers in the bar around the corner play "Paper Doll" slow and blue. After a moment Stanley comes out of the bathroom dripping water and still in his wet polka dot drawers. He calls for Stella. When he receives no answer he assumes that she has left him. He breaks into sobs. Then he goes to the telephone and dials a number. Eunice answers but refuses to let him speak with Stella. Shuddering with sobs, he stumbles out onto the porch to the side of the building. Standing half naked in the pale light of the moon, he throws back his head and bellows his wife's name: "Stell-lah h h h."

Finally, from out of the darkness at the top of the stairs comes his wife and tears are streaming from her eyes. Stanley meets Stella with an animal embrace, lifts her and carries her into their apartment. Blanche comes out of the upstairs looking for Stella. Mitch appears from around the corner and tells her everything is fine, Stella has gone back to Stanley. Defeated and confused Blanche sits down on the steps to have a cigarette with Mitch. He is tender and kind, and Blanche begins to realize that Mitch may offer the kindness she needs.

SUMMARY

In this scene we realize the following points:

1. The conflict between Stanley and Blanche is coming to a head. Blanche shows her tremendous potential by succeeding in creating a fight between Stella and Stanley. However, in the end she comes out the loser.

2. There is a strong tie between Stella and Stanley. It is, however, only physical and can be broken. The substance of their marriage is being supported by a very tenuous foundation.

3. Blanche, again, depends upon the kindness of Mitch to give her stability and reason in a difficult and confusing world.

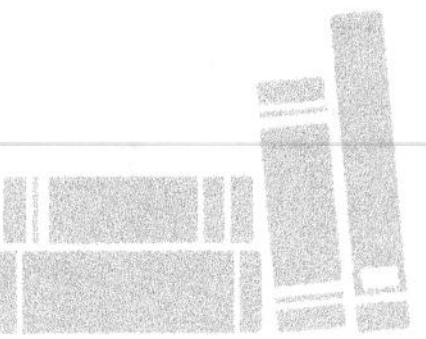

A STREETCAR NAMED DESIRE

TEXTUAL ANALYSIS

SCENES 4 - 11

SCENE FOUR

It is early the following morning. The brilliance of the morning sun acts as an antiseptic to the disease of last night's **episode** Stanley has gone out and Stella is lying comfortably and serenely on an unmade bed. The table in the kitchen still shows signs of the previous night's poker party. Blanche appears at the door. She has spent a sleepless night and her appearance entirely contrasts with Stella's. She looks nervously through the door. Seeing Stella on the bed, she rushes to her in a state of hysterical tenderness. After what happened, she cannot understand how Stella can return to her husband. Stella tries to explain to Blanche that Stanley frequently acts that way when he has been drinking too much. She recalls that on their wedding night, Stanley broke all the light bulbs with the heel of her slipper. Blanche shows very little patience with this type of behavior. She tries to persuade Stella that she is married to a madman. She considers Stella's situation in life worse than her own, because Stella refuses to face facts. Stella tells Blanche that she is quite content with her situation because it is one of her own making. Blanche refuses to be convinced. She tells Stella of a plan that will help them both. Determined that money would satisfy all their ills, Blanche recalls an old admirer of hers, Shep Huntleigh, who has become a millionaire in Texas' oil wells. She decides to telegraph him for money, then realizing that won't work, she becomes confused and starts to ramble on about Stanley. She says that she can't live in the same house with him after last night. She can understand Stella's position, she can live with him because she is married to him, but all Stanley has to offer is brute animal satisfaction. Being a product of Belle Reve, she cannot understand how Stella can be seduced by such a desire. Desire was the name of the streetcar that brought her there and it was desire that also attracted Stella. One is a conveyance, the other is a craving and there must be a difference. As Blanche continues to talk, Stanley enters unnoticed and stands motionless by the door. He overhears Blanche describe him as "common," "bestial," and "ape like." She pictures him in the cave age, coming home with meat over his shoulder to a wife who waits upon his every whim, and in the evening the rest of the apes gather for a poker party. She contrasts this with all of the good things that Stella was taught to appreciate at Belle Reve; art, poetry, music and the ways of a gentleman. She ends with a plea to Stella not to "hang back with the brutes." Still unnoticed, Stanley turns and walks back out the door. Once again on the outside, he calls to Stella. She runs to the door to meet him and in full view of Blanche they embrace with fierce, animal intensity. The light fades with a lingering brightness on their embrace. And as the sound of the "blue piano" rises in the background the scene ends.

SUMMARY

The importance of this scene is expressed in Blanche's desperate effort to regain her position of dominance over Stella, once her little sister. She was completely shattered by Stella's return to her husband. Her nervousness, her indecision, her strong contempt for Stanley, are signs of desperation. She is now in great need of assurance that her traditional way of life is the only respectable life. She shows contempt for Stanley, but her constant reference to his animal prowess indicates a strong fascination and subconscious desire. Blanche is becoming aware of this and she is frightened.

SCENE FIVE

A few days later. As the scene opens we see Blanche amused by a letter she has just written to Shep Huntleigh. In the letter she tells him that she is spending the summer visiting friends and it "has been a continued round of entertainments, teas, cocktails, and luncheons." Suddenly a disturbance is heard from the flat above. Eunice and her husband Steve are having a row. Then, Eunice runs out and down the stairs threatening to call the police. Shortly after she rounds the corner of the building Stanley makes an entrance. He walks into his apartment just as Steve comes down the steps looking for his wife. Stanley tells him she can be found at the corner bar getting a drink. Blanche observes this entire **episode** with smug righteousness. She makes a cynical reference to the language used and comments on Stanley's habit of banging things around. She is riding high at the top of her form when Stanley asks if she is acquainted with a man named Shaw. Blanche becomes pale and quiet as Stanley reveals that Shaw thinks he met her in Laurel, the town in which

Blanche taught school. Shaw travels in and out of Laurel quite often and stays at the Hotel Flamingo. Blanche vigorously denies that she knows the man, for the Hotel Flamingo is not the sort of establishment she would dare to be seen in. Stanley admits that he might be mistaken, but he will check out the facts with Shaw. Blanche becomes nervous and faint, her hands begin to tremble.

When Stanley leaves she confronts Stella with questions. She is anxious to know if Stella has heard any gossip about her. Stella is surprised to hear Blanche ask such a question. But Blanche feels she must admit to Stella that there was a good deal of talk about her in Laurel. She blames it on the fact that she is getting older, and a person who is faced with advancing age without a husband must make herself attractive. Stella, not understanding her sister's dilemma, refuses to listen. Blanche changes the subject to Mitch. She wants Mitch to like her, but she refuses to sacrifice her virtue to get him. Not that Mitch has made improper advances, but on the other hand men lose interest quickly. Blanche has not told him her real age, she is afraid he will take exception to it and her vanity has already suffered a great deal. She wants Mitch because she wants to rest and breathe quietly again and to live in a place of her own. Stella assures her sister that that day will come. Then, upon hearing Stanley call from the outside, she kisses Blanche and leaves.

The lights are dim, for it is evening now. Blanche settles down in a chair with a drink of liquor mixed with coke. There is a glimmer of lighting seen about the building as a young man approaches the apartment door. He has come to collect for the newspaper. Blanche asks him to come in and offers him a drink, a strange look of joy has come into her face. The young man refuses the drink and cautiously tells her that if she doesn't have the money he can come back later. Blanche forces herself on him by asking a light for her cigarette. As the young man complies,

Blanche continues her flirtation. She calls him a "Prince out of the Arabian Nights." The young man laughs uncomfortably and stands like a bashful kid. Uninhibited from the drink of liquor, Blanche kisses him. She then tells him to run along for she must "keep my hands off children." The young man departs hastily. Blanche is standing at the door as Mitch appears around the corner with a bunch of roses. She accepts the flowers gracefully and with great dignity, as the scene ends.

SUMMARY

During this scene a good deal more of Blanche's character is revealed. We realize that the nervousness and anxiety she feels is caused by something in her past life. Up until this scene she has presented herself as the perfect young lady, with the exception of her taste for liquor. Now her puritanical facade is beginning to crack. She becomes ludicrous and pathetic in her desperate attempt to maintain self-control.

SCENE SIX

It is later the same evening. Blanche and Mitch are just returning from an amusement park. As the audience sees them, in a dim blue glow of light, it is obvious that they are both weary from physical exhaustion. They stop outside the apartment door while Blanche looks for her key. Noticing that the hour is late, Blanche asks Mitch how he plans on getting home. Mitch informs her that the streetcar named Desire is still running. Sensing Blanche's fatigue, Mitch observes that the evening was uneventful. He attempts to apologize to Blanche but she takes the blame herself. With the intention of leaving, Mitch asks Blanche if he may kiss her good night. Blanche taunts him about his habit of asking for a kiss. She would prefer that he just kiss her; however, it is the other little familiarities that she tends to discourage. She wants him to understand that a girl alone in the world has got to keep a firm hold on her emotions or she'll be lost. It is obvious that Mitch is attracted by this show of reserved emotions so Blanche invites him into the apartment. She decides to leave the lights off so they may delight in a drink by candlelight. She begins to create a scene of amour. Mitch begins to talk about himself and Blanche compliments his looks, his weight, and his strength. As he attempts to show his strength by lifting her, Blanche cautions him to behave. She again asserts herself as having "old-fashioned ideals." Mitch then changes the subject to Stanley and Stella. He suggests that the four of them go out together some evening. Blanche is repulsed by the idea. She plays on Mitch's sympathy by telling him how cruelly she has been treated by Stanley. Mitch finds this hard to believe, but Blanche's intention has worked and he feels very close to her now. He tells her of his mother, who would like to see her son married and settled down before she dies. Realizing that Mitch feels great devotion for his mother, Blanche senses the loneliness he would experience after her death. For loneliness has had a great effect on Blanche's life. She reveals to Mitch the story of the only man she has ever loved. She was sixteen when she first discovered love, and she married a boy who was gentle, tender, and handsome. She soon discovered she had been deluded. Too late she found out her husband was a homosexual. He came to her for help, but not understanding his affliction she taunted him unmercifully. One evening while dancing to the music of the Varsouviana he suddenly broke from the floor and ran out of the casino. A few moments later a shot was heard. The boy, unable to bear her scorn, committed suicide. His death was a terrible shock to Blanche for she loved him unendurably, and from that day on the light of the world has been no brighter than the flame of a candle. As she finishes her story Mitch takes her in his arms and kisses her. They both realize their need for each other as Blanche whispers softly, "sometimes-there's God-so quickly.!"

SUMMARY

The construction of this scene is most interesting: it begins with Blanche's planned intention of seducing and winning Mitch. It ends with an expression of true and sincere emotion and an understanding of Blanche and Mitch's real need for each other. The scene reveals Blanche's basic needs and desires to be truly honorable, and that the tragedy lies in her inability to find satisfaction without sacrificing her honor. Also, the episode with the newspaper boy becomes understandable when we correlate it with Blanche's experience with a young husband.

SCENE SEVEN

It is late afternoon in mid-September. A table is set for a birthday supper with cake and flowers. Stella is completing the decorations as Stanley enters. He inquires about the preparations and is told that it is Blanche's birthday. He becomes irritated when he hears that Blanche is soaking in a hot tub on a day with the temperature of 100 degrees. Stella senses that something more important is bothering Stanley and forces him to reveal it. He tells her he has spent the past two months checking on Blanche and he is now prepared to prove she has been lying. Blanche's singing can be heard coming from the bathroom as Stanley unfolds his evidence. He has found that Blanche is not the prim and proper lady that she pretends to be. News of her reputation in Laurel exceeds that of the President of the United States, only not as well respected. Stanley has discovered that the Hotel Flamingo, a second-class hotel that pays little attention to the social life of their guests, was Blanche's home after the loss of Belle Reve. Her activities there became so disreputable that the management requested her to turn in her room key-permanently. This took place just a couple of weeks before she arrived in New Orleans. She has also been noted for her associations with soldiers from an army camp outside Laurel. Stanley also discovered that Blanche did not take a leave of absence from her position at that high school. They kicked her out before the term was over because of her intimacies with a seventeen-year-old student. As Stanley finishes his long lurid tale of investigation Stella is dumbfounded. She tells him his information is false, or at best half-truths. She admits that Blanche has always been flighty, but this was because of the disappointment she suffered from her young marriage. Stanley had no patience or sympathy with Blanche's early life. He asks Stella if anyone else is invited for the birthday party. She tells him that Mitch is coming for cake and coffee, but as she turns to look at Stanley she fears the worst. Stanley had told Mitch about Blanche and he will not be coming. Stella is disheartened. She had hoped for Mitch to marry Blanche; now what will Blanche do? Stanley tells her that Blanche will be leaving on Tuesday, for a birthday present he bought Blanche a one-way bus ticket back to Laurel. Blanche enters from the bathroom with gay expectation, but as she looks in to the face of Stanley and Stella she realizes something has happened. She stares fearfully at Stella as the scene ends.

SUMMARY

In this scene we realize, more vividly, the character of Blanche. We also have a greater understanding of the conflict between Stanley and Blanche; Blanche is repulsed by Stanley's manners, and behavior, but at the same time, because of her past experiences, she is attracted by his masculinity. We also see that Stanley is insistent upon getting rid of Blanche because of the disruption she has caused in his household. Like all men, and animals, he looks for security in his own home.

SCENE EIGHT

A short time later the birthday supper is over. Blanche still has hope that Mitch will arrive. Stanley is sullen and quiet. Stella is embarrassed and sad. Blanche is trying to make small talk, but she is unsuccessful. She prevails upon Stanley to tell a funny story, but he declines stating that she would not be interested in any story he would have to tell. She attempts a story of her own about a preacher and a parrot that cursed a blue streak. Stanley responds by eating another pork chop with his fingers. Stella is disgusted by her husband's behavior. She asks him to help clear the table. With one sweep of his hand, Stanley hurls the dishes to the floor and announces "the table is cleared." Then he turns on his wife and Blanche and declares that he is fed up with their attitude toward him, he demands respect in his own home for "every man is a king and I am the king around here, so don't you forget it." Stella begins to cry. Stanley stalks out of the door. Blanche, well aware that something is wrong, demands enlightenment from Stella. Stella refuses and walks out onto the porch. Blanche then goes to the phone and calls Mitch. Finding that he is not at home, she slumps into a chair, frightened. On the porch, Stanley approaches his wife repentantly. He assures her that soon everything will be all right. Stella, resigned to her duty toward her husband, accompanies him back into the apartment. While Stella is lighting the birthday candles Blanche enters from the bedroom. Stanley announces that he has a birthday gift and Blanche is delightfully embarrassed. The Varsouviana music is heard in the distance as Blanche opens the gift and finds a ticket back to Laurel. She is stunned. Suddenly she runs out of the room. Then they hear sounds of coughing and gagging coming from the bathroom. Stella is weak with pity and embarrassment. She turns on her husband and accuses him and all the men like him of having forced Blanche into her present condition. Stanley tries to ignore his wife's ranting, but Stella demands a reason for his cruel behavior toward Blanche. Stanley, in a fit of final revenge, boasts to Stella how he, a commoner, pulled her down off the columns of her aristocratic estates and made her love it. While he is speaking, Stella feels the beginning of pain. She quietly looks at her husband and asks to be taken to the hospital. Stanley, sobered by the thought of fatherhood, leads his wife to the door as the scene ends.

SUMMARY

In this scene is seen the beginning of Blanche's total destruction. She has nowhere to turn. All avenues of escape or comfort have been cut off. She still has a slight hope of being rescued by Mitch, but she is fearful that he also will reject her. Stanley has won the battle. His wife is now bound to him for the dependence of a newborn child.

SCENE NINE

It is later in the evening. Blanche is seen seated in a chair in the bedroom. She has been drinking, the bottle of liquor and a glass sit on a table next to her. In the background can be heard the rapid, feverish polka tune, the "Varsouviana." The music is in her mind; she has been drinking to escape it and the sense of disaster closing in on her, and she seems to whisper the words of the song. Suddenly, Mitch appears from around the corner. He is unshaven and dressed in his working clothes. He knocks at the door. Blanche is startled. She calls out to discover who it is. When she hears Mitch reply, she becomes desperately excited. She hides the bottle of liquor, powders her face, then hurries to the door. She plays coy when she sees him, but Mitch brushes by her and stalks into the room. In an effort to maintain her composure, Blanche acts tolerant and forgiving. Mitch sits on the bed and lights a cigarette. Blanche offers him a drink, but he refuses on the grounds that it belongs to Stanley. Blanche is afraid to ask Mitch why he came so late, she is just pleased that he came. He stopped the music of the "Varsouviana" from running through her mind. While Blanche is looking for another bottle of liquor, Mitch tells her he had not planned on coming tonight. Blanche pretends not to hear this, but finds the liquor. When she returns to the room Mitch has his foot on the bed. Blanche, feeling this as a sign of disrespect, asks him to remove his foot. She, again, offers him a drink and he, for the second time, refuses it. He then tells Blanche that she has been lapping up liquor all summer long like a "wild-cat." Blanche winces at this remark, but struggles to maintain her poise. Mitch then complains about the darkness of the room and recalls that Blanche always wants it dark when he is with her. She even refused to go out with him on a Sunday afternoon. Blanche admits that she likes darkness. Mitch decides to get a good look at Blanche. She becomes frightened as he rips the paper lantern off the light hanging in the middle of the room and turns on the switch. Blanche cries out and covers her face. Mitch realizes that Blanche is older than he thought, but he tells her this doesn't matter as much as the lies she has been telling him about her past. She asks where he got his information. He verified Stanley's stories, he tells her, by talking with three men, all of whom knew her. Blanche recognizes the names. The moment she feared most has arrived. She does not try to refute his proof, she is too numb for that.

With the feeling that there is nothing more to save in her relationship with Mitch, Blanche drops all pretense. In a rage of shame and abandonment she flaunts her adventurous past before her gawking suitor. She tells him she had many intimacies after the death of her husband-it was the only way "to fill an empty heart." In a fit of convulsive, sobbing laughter she relates the story of the seventeen-year-old student and her dismissal as a person "morally unfit for her position." She confesses that she came to New Orleans looking for sanctuary from a future that looked no more promising than her degenerate past. When she met Mitch she found hope, she recognized the pains of loneliness that can be smoothed by two people in need of each other. But her past is too close behind and the moment she feared the most has caught up with her. Mitch, fumbling for words, repeats his accusation "you lied to me, Blanche." A Mexican Woman is seen coming around the corner of the building selling flowers. The music of the Varsouviana becomes louder. Blanche stands fixed with a glazed look in her eyes. Mitch stands and crosses to behind Blanche. He places his hands on her waist and tries to turn her about. Blanche, awakened to reality, asks Mitch to marry her. Mitch answers by telling her she is not clean enough to live in the same house with his mother, but he wants the same consideration that she has given other men. Blanche's voice tightens with hysteria as she forces Mitch from the apartment. She then staggers back from the door and falls to her knees. The music of the Varsouviana fades as the scene ends.

SUMMARY

It is realized now that Blanche is completely alone in the world. She has lost her last hope of survival in the rational world, she must now look for other means of escape. Mitch, also, is lost. He needs Blanche as desperately as she needs him for he must fight the loving domination of his mother.

However, he is not able to withstand the truth. He will never be needed as a man as much as he was by Blanche.

SCENE TEN

It is a short time later the same night. Blanche is standing by her open trunk dressed in a somewhat soiled and crumpled white satin evening gown and a pair of silver slippers. In the process of packing and drinking she has reached a state of juvenile make-believe. She is looking into a small hand mirror and talking to herself. Suddenly, she slams the mirror down on the top of the trunk with such violence that the glass cracks. A moan of despair is heard as she attempts to rise. Stanley appears around the corner of the building. He has had a few drinks on the way and has brought some bottles of beer home with him. He slams the door after entering the kitchen and, seeing Blanche dressed in her white satin gown, gives a low whistle. Blanche enquires about Stella and the baby. Stanley tells her the baby is not expected until morning, so they told him to go home and get some sleep. Blanche realizes that she and Stanley will be alone during the night. Stanley questions Blanche about the outfit she is wearing. Blanche announces that she has received an invitation from Shep Huntleigh to cruise on the Caribbean in a yacht. Stanley expresses a pretended surprise as he leads Blanche on with questions about Shep. In the meantime he removes his shirt as he looks for a bottle opener. Blanche is distressed by his half-nakedness and asks him to dress behind closed drapes. Stanley ignores her remark and opens a bottle of beer in a spray of foam. He offers one to Blanche, but she refuses. Then he continues to taunt her about her oil-millionaire. Blanche explains, defiantly, that Shep is a gentleman and holds a great deal of respect for her; he is just a lonely man who wants company. A woman with culture, intelligence, and breeding, she continues, does not need physical beauty to enrich a man's life. She chastises herself for possessing these virtues and yet being foolish enough to cast them like "pearls before swine." Stanley is impressed by the word "swine." Blanche tells him that she not only uses the word in reference to him but also his friend Mr. Mitchell, who charged in on her this evening spouting lies and vicious stories about her. She then tells Stanley how she sent him away only to have him return later with flowers and a sense of forgiveness. She would not accept his bribe, however, for "some things are not forgivable." Nothing was lost in her refusal, she admits, for they are totally incompatible. Stanley becomes cruel and indignant. He calls Blanche a liar. He does not believe the story about Shep Huntleigh, and he knows Mitch did not return with flowers because he knows where he is. Her whole life has been full of lies, conceit, and tricks, he tells her. Nevertheless, he has been on to her from the beginning, she has never once "pulled the wool over this boy's eyes." She has come into his house acting like a Queen and now he is fed up with her. Blanche pulls away startled as Stanley walks past her and into the bathroom. She reaches for the phone and asks the operator for long distance. She attempts to place a call to Shep Huntleigh, but finds that she doesn't know his address. Suddenly she turns and sees Stanley emerging from the bathroom in a pair of silk pajamas, the pair he wore on his wedding night. She pulls away from the phone stricken with fright. Stanley approaches her silently. Blanche feels her whole world slipping away from under her. She tries desperately to hold on to her sanity. She grabs a bottle and smashes it on the table, then turns facing Stanley with the broken end clutched in her hand, but this is not enough. Her world of reality is no more. She faints as Stanley struggles to free the broken bottle. He then picks up her inert body and carries her to the bed.

SUMMARY

This scene shows the final destruction of Blanche. She has lost her last contact with the outside world. Now, in order to find peace and security she must escape inwardly, into herself and create a world of her own making. For Stanley, the rape of Blanche is the culmination and symbol of victory. He had already dragged Stella down to the level of his own existence, then, being threatened by Blanche and her appearance of respectability, he was again challenged by the tradition of Belle Reve. He triumphed by proving that she is not as superior as she has seemed. For Stanley that was not enough. He must prove that the world is a pigsty and he is the king of pigs so he extends his victory to the point of total destruction for his adversary, Blanche.

SCENE ELEVEN

It is some weeks later. The four men-Stanley, Steve, Mitch and Pablo are sitting around the kitchen table playing poker. Stella is in the bedroom packing Blanche's things. She has tears in her eyes. In the background can be heard the splashing of water, coming from the bathroom. A strange solemnity is apparent in the scene. Eunice comes down the steps from the flat above and enters the kitchen. She is disgusted at the sight of men playing poker at a time like this. She then walks into the bedroom to help Stella with the packing. Stella enquires about her baby whom Eunice is caring for until the evening events are over. Eunice assures her their newly born son is sound asleep in the upstairs apartment. After a pause Eunice asks for Blanche. Stella points towards the bathroom. Stella has not told Blanche that she will be leaving this evening. She has made arrangements for Blanche to be taken to an institution. In her present state of mind, Blanche has the impression that she will be going for a cruise with Shep Huntleigh. She calls from the bathroom for Stella to check her clothing. Stella assures her that everything is in readiness. With tears streaming down her cheeks, Stella turns to Eunice and confesses that she has to send Blanche away for she could not allow herself to believe Blanche's story about Stanley. She could not believe it and continue to live with Stanley. Eunice tells her never to believe it for no matter what happens life must go on. Blanche enters and expresses grave disappointment that Shep has not called. Then Blanche hears Stanley's voice from the other room and suddenly, for one strange fleeting moment, she is shocked back to reality. Frantically she demands to know why Stella and Eunice stand staring at her with pity and sorrow on their faces. The moment passes and she once again becomes interested in preparations for her trip. Now she is anxious to leave, but Stella tells her to wait until the poker game breaks up. Not wanting to encounter the men on the way out, Blanche agrees. From around the corner of the building come a Doctor and a Matron. They climb the steps of the porch and ring the doorbell. Eunice glances fitfully at Stella and then crosses through the kitchen to answer the door. Blanche waits excitedly to hear if the caller is for her. Eunice returns and announces that the callers are for Blanche and they are waiting outside. Blanche immediately assumes that it is Shep Huntleigh, but is confused by the accompanying lady. She hurries to get ready. As Blanche passes through the kitchen Mitch is visibly affected. She steps out on the small porch at the side of the door and stops. She does not recognize the doctor as the man she was expecting. She suddenly gasps and starts back into the kitchen. Stella is at the door to block her way. There is a moment of silence-no sound but that of Stanley steadily shuffling the cards. Blanche catches her breath again and slips by Stella into the kitchen. As she heads for the bedroom Stanley stands in front of her. With a fury, she pushes past him and escapes into the bedroom. In response to Stanley's instruction, the Matron advances into the bedroom to bring Blanche out. With Stanley on one side and the Matron on the other, Blanche is trapped like an animal. They start to bait her. Stanley asks if she returned for her paper lantern which he rips off the light and holds out to her. Stella falls sobbingly into the arms of Eunice. Mitch, unable to contain himself any longer, charges at Stanley. Stanley pushes Mitch back over the table and Mitch lies there, sobbing. In the meantime the Matron has prevented Blanche from running by pinning her arms behind her back. Blanche lets out a mournful cry and falls to her knees. The doctor crosses to Blanche and signals for the Matron to release her. He then takes off his hat and crouches in front of her. As he speaks to Blanche his voice is gentle and reassuring. She turns and with a look of desperate pleading extends her hand to him. He draws her up gently and supports her with his arm as he leads her to the door. Blanche, with complete confidence tells the doctor she has "always depended on the kindness of strangers." As they pass, Stella cries out her sister's name, but Blanche walks on without turning. After they have left, Eunice descends the stairs and places Stella's child in her arms. Stella sobs insistently as Stanley approaches her timidly, with feeble words of comfort. In the kitchen we see Steve and Pablo continuing the poker game as the scene ends.

SUMMARY

In the final scene it is realized that Stanley does not escape without paying a price for his victory. He has completely destroyed Blanche, but he has also jeopardized his relationship with his wife. Stella exclaims that she cannot believe Blanche's story of the rape and still live with Stanley, but this does not mean that she entirely disbelieves her sister. She must make a choice and because of the dependency of her child she chooses Stanley. Nevertheless, memories of her stricken and defenseless sister being led away to an institution will always stand between her and Stanley.

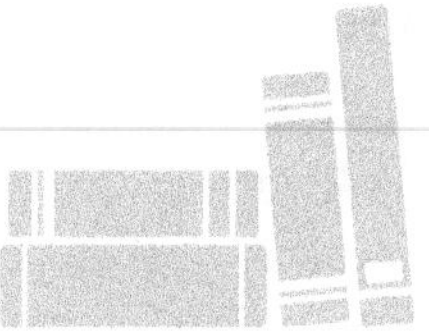

A STREETCAR NAMED DESIRE

CHARACTER ANALYSES

Blanche Dubois

Blanche DuBois is the culmination of many womanly characteristics in the repertoire of Tennessee Williams. She is first seen in a one-act play written in 1939 called *The Lady of Larkspur Lotion*. The story is about an abandoned forty-year-old blonde, Southern ex-belle who has degenerated into a prostitute. In order to defend herself against an insistent landlady and to cling to some shreds of respectability she invents a story about waiting for dividends from her rubber plantation in Brazil. Blanche Dubois is seen more clearly in *Portrait of a Madonna*, another one-act play written during Williams' earlier period in New Orleans. It is a sympathetic study of the mental deterioration of a Southern spinster. She is lost in a world of her own delusions. She imagines that she has finally won the young man that left her many years ago and that she is expecting his child. Toward the end of the play a Doctor and Nurse, performing their duty wearily but efficiently, come to take her away. The play closes as she is being led to the asylum by the doctor, who treats her with kindness and gallantry. Myra Torrance and Cassandra Whiteside in *Battle of Angels*, Matilda Rockley in *You Touched*

Me, Laura and Amanda Wingfield in *The Glass Menagerie*, and Alma Winemiller in *Summer and Smoke* are all identifiable in the fusion of characteristics that make up Blanche DuBois.

When Blanche arrives at the end of the line of the streetcar named Desire she is a desperate woman. She is desperate because she is a fugitive from a society that is deteriorating also. Her background is the life at Belle Reve, one from which she cannot escape without serious consequences. Her tradition made her a woman of importance. She felt secure within the function of her own society. Today that tradition no longer exists. It no longer works in our present society. Blanche, however, must believe in it, for without the tradition of Belle Reve, she cannot live; her whole life has been for nothing. She holds on to these shreds of Southern respectability, and by so doing she thinks she is performing an act of heroism, rather than absurd romanticism. Even the romantic **episode** with her young husband, who was tender, gentle, and sensitive, and whose tragic flaw was his sexual perversion, gives stature to her heroic character. She becomes one who is more to be pitied than censured because of her juvenile misunderstanding of her husband's need. By believing in her traditional background, Blanche finds an excuse for a great deal of her behavior. The present society rejects her as an **anachronism** and therefore, makes her feel alone and insecure. When the strength of her belief in tradition weakens, she looks for security in drink and the human warmth of contract with strangers. This is a sacrifice, however, for she must meet them on their terms and forget her own. Since she cannot fully accept her actions she begins to forget them. She creates a world of fantasy wherein she can rationalize her behavior as being the result of an unprotected, sensitive and delicate nature. In doing this she avoids facing the reality of her real physical and sensual desires. Her tradition will not allow her to accept such feelings as other than "brutal desire" and to give vent to them is sinful. Nevertheless, she does give vent to her feelings out of loneliness and an agonizing realization that her attraction for men is beginning to fade. She is on the brink of middle age and is desperately in a hurry to find a man. Like most women, Blanche is dependent upon a man for protection, for security, and for love. Because of her background, she also has a great need for someone to defend and maintain her honor. She is looking for someone who does not exist in the New Orleans environment to which she has come-a gentleman. She wants an old-fashioned wedding dressed in white with music, poetry, art and people with tender feelings, and not to be held back with the "brute desire" that make such things impossible. So she is constantly in conflict, and out of this comes frustration and a need for protection. That is what a woman of tradition needs, protection from an alien world that is passing her by and to which she is unable to adjust. That is why she comes to Stella and Stanley. She comes as a beaten individual who is drowning in a mire of degeneracy, but, because she is proud, she must make one last attempt. She, once again, draws upon an impotent tradition to make herself superior. Stanley, mistakenly, interprets her demeanor as a challenge to his basic existence as a man. Because of his strong connection with reality, he is able to destroy her. Blanche, therefore, destroys herself because of her foolish insistence of living with the illusions of the past. In the meantime, however, she has one stroke of luck. She finds someone who needs her as badly as she needs him, Mitch. For a short time she lives in happy anticipation, but her past catches up with her. With no one left to turn to for protection she takes refuge in fantasy. She becomes insane.

Stanley Kowalski

When the audience first sees Stanley Kowalski they see him as a personification of what Blanche later describes as a "sub-human, ape-like survivor of the stone age." One who bears meat home from the kill in the jungle and throws it down in front of his mate, who is waiting for him at the entrance to their abode. He might strike her or he might kiss her, depending upon his whim. In the evening the rest of the apes gather and they have an ape poker party with "grunting and swilling and gnawing and hulking." Stanley is like an animal who operates on essentially one dimension-the sensual. His life has been unpretentious and a matter of the survival of the fittest. His manners, speech, and appearance are all basic but sufficient to maintain life. However, he is different in the sense that he has a will and a desire to become more than just a common animal, he wants to become king, at least in his own home. If he can't become king, he will make sure that no one else gets ahead of him. Stanley can handle men because he believes in luck. He came out of the battle of Salerno with the odds four to five against him because he was lucky-"to hold front position in this rat-race, you've got to believe you are lucky." Stanley can handle women, too, although they are a little more complicated and, at times, little more difficult. He has sufficient physical potential to pull them down to his level and make them enjoy it, or to destroy them. Stanley takes pride in the domain he has built in his household and he also takes satisfaction in the security that it gives him. Pride and satisfaction are his two most prized possessions and when either is threatened he will fight with all of his animal instinct.

When Blanche first arrives at his apartment in New Orleans Stanley is suspicious of her. She comes from the same background as his wife and when Stella first saw Stanley she considered him common. Stanley was successful in toppling her from the white columns, which were symbolic of Belle Reve; will he be just as successful with Blanche? His main object, as Blanche first walks through the door, is to overcome her sexually for this is the way he won his wife. Regardless of what else might happen he will only truly be satisfied when he subdues her with his manly prowess. Blanche proves to be a more difficult adversary than Stanley had anticipated. Her formation in the depth of Belle Reve tradition was much more complete than Stella's. She insists upon the recognition of her time-honored habits and manners so strenuously that Stanley becomes suspicious of her motives. Driven by the fear of Blanche as a potential menace to his home, as a danger to his relationship with his wife, and as an object of sensuality that he may not be able to seduce, he sets out on his plan of destruction. Although Stanley is crude and powerful, he is not a fool. He is an animal that is in tune with nature and he finds that he can survive well in his jungle of men because he is more instinctively an animal than they are. He is the king among apes as long as he knows what the rest of the apes are thinking, and what makes them tick. He digs into Blanche's background looking for dirt, because to him all people are dirty. He recognizes it when he finds it, and he wallows in it because it is so much a part of him. Under another circumstance the sordidness of Blanche's life would be taken in stride. But Stanley has been made to realize the importance of his information by Blanche's insistence on playing the perfect young lady. When he attacks, he does it with all the cunning of a bestial marauder. He stalks his prey by telling Stella his findings and making sure that she will not interfere with his final attack. Then to prove his capability and strike terror in the heart of his adversary, he confronts her directly. He tells Blanche that he is on to her tricks and that she is nothing but a liar and a phony, and incapable of fighting with other animals, because she has never admitted to being a beast herself. He adds that he has cut off her only means of escape by telling Mitch about her past life. Not believing him she runs in the direction of this last avenue of hope only to find that escape is impossible. Trapped, defeated, and defenseless, Blanche becomes vulnerable to physical attack. Driven by his need to satisfy a desire that became evident the first moment he saw her, Stanley attacks viciously and devours every remaining morsel of respectability.

Stella Kowalski

Stella is Blanche's younger sister. She was brought up in the shadow of her older sister among the traditions of Belle Reve. Her parents, grandparents, uncles and aunts were part of a decaying Southern aristocracy and they spent all of their energies on trying to maintain their social position. The two sisters were very close and Blanche felt the responsibility of raising Stella. Together they learned to appreciate art, music, poetry, and the manners of Southern gentlemen. Being an older sister had its advantages: Blanche could command Stella to wait on her, to arrange her clothes when preparing for a ball or a carriage ride in the countryside. Because she felt the responsibilities of an older sister, Blanche affected a superior attitude, which caused an unconscious hostility in the mind of her sister. As Stella grew older she began to feel the pressures of her sister's domination and a lack of obligation to a disintegrating heritage. She looked for an escape and found one in the person of Stanley Kowalski. Because of a rebellious attitude fostered within her, she was willing to overlook any seeming appearance of outward respectability. Boredom and uncertainty gave way to happiness and womanhood without Stella really knowing why. She hesitated to investigate for fear that a world of pleasure would be taken from her. Stanley gives her joy and contentment in the world in which they live and this narcotic world will remain the same as long as neither one seeks to change it. The life that Stanley offers is completely satisfying to one who will live it according to his terms, and Stella has accepted these terms. She lives in a sensual stupor. She shuts out all challenge all day long. She loafs, does her hair, her nails, fixes a dress, doesn't eat much, but prepares Stanley's dinner and waits for Stanley. She hopes for no other meaning from life. Stanley has awakened her to her physical self as she never expected to be awakened; with him she realizes herself as a woman.

She is in a paradise, serenely limited paradise, when Blanche enters. Blanche immediately poses a threat to Stella's existence. She makes her consider Stanley in a different light, one that is reflective of the "gentlemen" they knew back in Mississippi. Stella is made to judge Stanley for the first time and, although she refuses to admit it, he is found wanting. Her reasons for marrying Stanley are now put on trial, because Blanche's presence causes her to revert to her former values. Her sympathies go out to Blanche because of her tragic marriage, and she tries to shield her from Stanley. Stella's doubts and fears erupt into open conflict for the first time on the evening of the poker party. Seeing Stanley drunk and disorderly disgusts her. Blanche's visions of apes and sub-humans come vividly to mind, as she rushes out the door after Stanley's blows hurt more in her mind than on her body. However, Stella realizes that without Stanley, she too might become a pathetic caricature of a fading Southern aristocrat. So no matter what Stanley does she must cling to him, as to life itself. When Stanley cries out for her, Stella rushes back into his arms. Later, when Blanche tells her about the rape, she must pretend that Blanche is mad to avoid losing Stanley. However, Stella is doomed too. She had settled for a temporary solution. She has denied a great part of her life just to live for Stanley's pleasures, but she cannot live drugged forever. She is much more of a human being than that. Eventually her life with Stanley will wear thin and her only hope will be her children. Like so many women she will start living more and more for her children. Blanche, despite apparent failure, makes Stella realize certain things about Stanley. At the end of the play, her life is entirely different. It will never be the same with Stanley again.

Harold (Mitch) Mitchell

Mitch is the disappointing hero of the play. When his character first becomes realized the audience sees him as a big, tough, burly fellow with a rough Southern voice and the manner of a homespun, awkward, overgrown boy. He is gentle and kind and sees Blanche as a real person, one to be respected and listened to. He seems capable and willing to understand the loneliness of other people because he has known loneliness himself. He and Blanche seem to be made for each other because they both have a fidelity to the roots from which they sprang. Mitch has a true devotion to his mother, he provides and cares for her and she in turn sets the standards by which he lives. Blanche also has true devotion to her childhood, and it in turn sets the standards by which she must live. Mitch needs Blanche as an escape from the conflicts that have arisen because of his gentlemanliness in a hostile environment: he is embarrassed by his poker-playing buddies who criticize him for being a momma's boy. Because he is no longer a boy he feels a need to prove his manliness, and a means by which he can satisfy his desires. Blanche is ideal for him. He can take her home and his mother will be proud of him and still she has the potential of satisfying his physical desires. In his relationship with Blanche he has finally found a girl who needs him, and he knows this is an important moment in his life to prevent a future of loneliness. Blanche needs Mitch, also, as an escape from the hostility of her environment. He is a caricature of a Southern gentleman, and yet, curiously, he is a gentleman. She needs Mitch for security, warmth, and protection of her honor. Mitch needs Blanche as desperately as she needs him. Then why did Mitch reject her in the end? There is a difference in the backgrounds of Mitch and Blanche, an important difference. By a quirk of fate, Blanche was cast out of her juvenile environment into a world that was alien to her. Although she found this world full of conflict and difficulty, she benefited by her exposure to reality. She understood the depths of sorrow and despair, and the degradation that can be caused by an inability to cope with such emotions. She had a keen awareness of the desperate fight a person must wage to prevent loneliness. However, she was unable to adjust to this type of reality and so she was destroyed. Mitch has never experienced life free from the protection of his mother. Neither by fate nor as the result of his own doing has he had the opportunity of facing up to reality. His responses to pity, sorrow, loneliness, are all conditioned by the tutoring of his mother. Although he can recognize the results of emotion in people he can never truly understand its cause. So when he was finally faced with the bawdy truth of reality his response was conditional, he ran to avoid confusion. Mitch will always be the big boy because he failed his test for manliness. In the environment of the New Orleans slums, Mitch's lack of manliness will eventually destroy him.

Eunice and Steve Hubbell

The Hubbells are the owners of the building in which the Kowalskis live. Steve is the prototype of Stanley. He lives his life and treats his wife in the same manner as does Stanley, only when he hits her she strikes back. Eunice is older than Stella and much wiser in the ways of living in the slums of New Orleans. She is content with her situation because she has learned to accept life for what it is and for whatever happens "life has got to go on."

Stella uses Eunice as a model of conformity to a life that was completely foreign to her. With Eunice's help and advice Stella not only endures the day by day existence with Stanley, but she also enjoys it. Unlike Blanche, Eunice offers no recognition of the better things in life and Stella can continue to live her narcotized existence with Stanley without the feelings of guilt.

Eunice and Steve have developed a harmony in their marital life that is envied by Stella and Stanley. They present an important example to follow if Stella and Stanley's marriage is to remain successful.

Negro Woman and Pablo Gonzalez

Tennessee Williams uses the characters of the Negro Woman and Pablo as a representation of the integrated neighborhood in which the Kowalskis live. New Orleans is a cosmopolitan city where there is a relatively warm and easy intermingling of races in the old section of the town.

Young Man

The Young Man is a symbolic image of one of Blanche's weaknesses. Her flirtation with him in **scene five** and the past history of Blanche's seduction of a seventeen-year-old boy are explained by her tragic marriage to a young man, Allan Grey.

Mexican Woman

The Mexican Woman enters in **scene nine** as a flower vendor. Her cry is "flores para los muertos" (flowers for the dead). It is in **scene nine** that Blanche realizes that Mitch no longer wants her and that all hope is gone. The vendor's cry becomes a symbolic **refrain** for the play.

Doctor and Nurse

In the very last moment of the play the two solemn figures of the Doctor and the Nurse enter to take Blanche away to the asylum. Blanche's reaction to their individual approaches is indicative of her reaction to life. The Nurse approaches Blanche with harshness and physical cruelty and Blanche reacts vehemently, as she did to Stanley and the rest of the crudeness in the world. The Doctor approaches Blanche with tenderness and gentility and she responds favorably for she has "always depended on the kindness of strangers."

Commentary

"It said everything I had to say," was Tennessee Williams' comment on his play *A Streetcar Named Desire*. After undergoing an operation that resulted in the removal of three inches of small intestine, Williams was convinced that his next play would be his last. He set out to explore the far recesses of his mind to establish his main philosophy of life, "The apes shall inherit the earth." Williams was a very sickly and sensitive person in his youth and very easily subjected to the harshness and cruelty of others. In *A Streetcar Named Desire* it is obvious that he regards most men as savages and that his sympathies lie with the sensitive, gentle, unprotected recipient of the world's cruelty, who intends not to "hang back with the brutes!" Therefore, Randolph Goodman feels that the play can "thus be read as an allegorical representation of the author's view of the world he lives in."

Most critics felt *A Streetcar Named Desire* to be a superior play to *The Glass Menagerie*, which at the time of the opening of *Streetcar* was the only other notable play the playwright had written. They recognized a distinctive talent and were intrigued by the scope and the complexity of the play. Brooks Atkinson in his review of the stage production found the play "almost unbearably tragic." The audience, he reported, came away "profoundly moved. . . . For they have been sitting all evening in the presence of truth, and that is a rare and wonderful experience." However, he made a subtle exception in the case of Blanche when he said: "Since she is created on the stage as a distinct individual, experiences identical with hers can never be repeated. She and the play that is woven about her are unique." Severe criticism has been made of the sensational moments of the play; the beating of Stella and the violation of Blanche, but Joseph Wood Krutch feels that, in spite of the sensational quality of the story, "the author's perceptions remain subtle and delicate and he is amazingly aware of nuances even in situations where nuance might seem to be inevitably obliterated by violence." He believed Williams' stories "enable him to communicate emotions which have special, personal significance," and that "his plays will be immediately recognizable by their familiar **themes** and a sensibility as unique as that of a lyric poet." To substantiate Krutch's remarks one has only to consider the method by which Williams handles the poetic overtones in *Streetcar*. Elia Kazan, broadway director, identifies this play as "poetic tragedy" and yet a strong reality of character, environment and dialogue is undeniably evident. We see the justification of Kazan's statement in the character of Blanche. Her traditional background abounds in refinement of language, manners, and education. Her present conditions of alcoholism, incontinence, and common prostitution are a drastic departure from all of the righteousness of her youth. In order to live with the knowledge of this social and physical degradation, Blanche must conceal her outward appearance with the affectations of a Southern lady. "Her consuming need, moreover, is to make herself and others constantly aware of her refinements," Gassner states. The memories of her past, however, are just as unbearable as her present circumstances so she must create a dream world of delusion, which becomes apparent in her outward behavior. She becomes a caricature of stylized manners and speech which encompasses the poetic quality of the play.

Thus, it becomes apparent that the poetic behavior of her past life is in conflict with the reality of her present life and, therefore, John Gassner observes that "In *Streetcar*, poetic drama becomes psychological reality." This fusion of the world of fantasy with the world of reality is important in the development of the main conflict of the play.

Blanche's opposition to the situation in which she is involved, as pointed out by John Gassner, creates a series of ambiguities. When she first arrives in the Kowalski household she is looking for a means of escape. She needs protection from a world to which she will not adjust. In seeking this protection, however, she refuses to realize her incongruity and benefit by her past mistakes. She insists that her way of life is the only correct way to live and, thereby causes a threat to the relationship between Stanley and Stella. It becomes evident that her stubborn insistence will shatter the very protection she seeks. Also, her insistence on the correct way of living is based upon a myth. Her previous life is nothing but a representation of a decayed society, one that has become extinct because of its refusal to adjust to modern times. Stella, who was reared in a similar tradition, made an attempt to adjust to modern society. It was a faulty adjustment, however, caused by a desperate need to escape the destruction of a rapidly disintegrating family heritage. Blanche, on the other hand, made no attempt to adjust and the result has been the destruction of not only her own life, but the lives of those whom she needed most, Stanley, Stella, and Mitch. Thus it appears that Blanche is the villain of the piece. When she first arrives she does nothing to commend herself. She drinks, she quarrels, she is superficial, and we can hardly wait for Stanley to tell her off. However, her adversary seems to fare no better in the hands of the playwright; Stanley is portrayed as the personification of disgusting normality, or as one of the brutes who will eventually inherit the earth. Stella is also pictured as one of the weaknesses rather than the strengths of civilization in her acceptance of a husband who gives her satisfaction of physical desires in lieu of a healthy social relationship. Nancy Tischner suggests that "apparently Williams wants the audience to believe that Stella is wrong in loving Stanley but right in living with him." With whom does the sympathy of the audience lie? Joseph Wood Krutch tries to clarify this ambiguity by making reference to a statement by Blanche in **scene two** while speaking to Stella about Stanley: "he's just not the type that goes for jasmine perfume, but maybe he's what we need to mix with our blood now that we've lost Belle Reve." Taking into consideration that Stella represents the decaying aristocracy and Stanley the natural man, Mr. Krutch answers that "virility, even orgiastic virility, is the proper answer to decadence." So the decaying aristocracy is rejuvenated by its union with a "representative of the people." Whereas part of the audience is in sympathy with Stella, the other part will share sympathy with Blanche in feeling "better decadence than this obscene surrender." Mr. Krutch, in appraising Blanche, insists, "Her instincts are right. She is on the side of civilization and refinement. But the age has placed her in a tragic dilemma. She looks about for a tradition according to which she may live and a civilization to which she can be loyal. She finds none. Ours is a society which has lost its shape." Behind Blanche lies a past which seems to have been civilized. "The culture of the Old South is dead, and she has good reason to know that it is. It is, however, the only culture about which she knows anything. The world of Stella and her husband is a barbarism-perhaps, as its admirers would say, a vigorous barbarism-but a barbarism nonetheless." In this dilemma, "Blanche chooses the dead past and becomes a victim of that impossible choice, but she does choose it rather than the 'adjustment' of her sister. At least she has not succumbed to barbarism." Thus we see the ambiguities are dramatically, indeed tragically, fruitful. The decision of the direction or division of sympathy lies entirely in the minds of the audience.

While Williams was successful in intensifying the dramatic interest in *Streetcar* with the use of ambiguity he, at the same time, caused confusion. John Gassner shows that he "reduced potential tragedy to psychopathology." Gassner diagnoses Blanche's psychological situation as "so untenable when she enters the home of Stanley and Stella that she should be receiving psychiatric care." Williams becomes improbable in his justification for the causes of many of Blanche's ills. Her background of the decline of an aristocratic family in the form of money, death, and morals and the tragic history of her marriage to a young sensitive homosexual hardly gives credibility to her own destruction. Despite the inefficiency of the stability of her early training, it is obvious that Blanche had received a good formal education. Her interest in the arts and her manner of conduct would warrant strong belief in her ability to make a reasonable living teaching school. The fact that a neurosis was caused by the suicide of her young maladjusted husband is a motivation found believable only in Williams' wild imagination. "Nor it is convincing," Mr. Gassner points out, "that the young husband's death should have led her to seduce school children and take up with soldiers in a neighboring camp. In *Streetcar*, in so far as Blanche's role is concerned, only her illness is believable-and even that is suspect, in so far as its inevitability is questionable." Blanche, then, although she has the intelligence, idealism, and tragic vision necessary for the classic heroine, falls short because psychopathology substitutes for Fate.

Williams intention of expressing the ills of the world in the brutish character of Stanley also smacks of dramatic excessiveness. In order to prove the validity of Stella's final decision of remaining faithful to Stanley, the ultimate and most important decision of the play, the audience must see proof of the fact that Stanley will make a good provider and father for her children. Initially it is apparent that Stanley has a great deal of confidence in himself as a man and a husband and that Stella can find security in his confidence. He can be admired for defending his home against the treachery of Blanche's influence and, for the sake of his own peace, to send her packing. But to justify the deliberate and brutal violation of Blanche on the pretense of dramatic effectiveness shows a basic weakness in the unity of the play. The audience is faced with the decision of whether Blanche and Stella's destruction was caused by their inability to adjust to the modern world or whether it was the result of a process of evolution that has succeeded in creating a society of monsters. Stanley is decidedly an abnormal member of society. His brutal attack on Blanche lowered him to a realm of degenerates who are in no way fit for society, much less to father children. Therefore, Stella's decision to choose her degenerate husband over an infirm sister lacks true motivation. In the case of Blanche, Mr. Gassner argues that if "the point of the play is precisely that Blanche, who needs every consideration, is thrust into a brute world that gives her no consideration, then, I say, Williams has destroyed the tragic possibilities of *Streetcar* in another way: He has settled for pathos whereas the ambience of his characterization of Blanche suggests a play possessed of a sharper, more equitable, and harder insight-namely, that of tragedy."

Was it Williams' intention to write "The Tragedy of Blanche DuBois," or was he more interested in proving man's inefficiency in obtaining completeness in our present-day society. Benjamin Nelson theorizes that "Blanche's inability to tragically mature is the direct result of her incompletion, her fragmentation, if you will. It is a fragmentation which manifests a greater and encompassing incompleteness in the universe itself." Here, Mr. Nelson alludes to a philosophy of the living as expressed by Tennessee Williams in his short story, "Desire and the Black Masseur."

In this tale Williams explains: "The nature of man is full of such makeshift arrangements, devised by himself to cover his incompletion. He feels a part of himself to be like a missing wall or a room left unfinished and he tries as well as he can to make up for it"; these are the sins of mankind. Mr. Nelson feels that Blanche is doomed because she cannot find complete satisfaction, precisely because Williams has not allowed the ingredients necessary to her satisfaction to exist in his created universe. Williams does not take into consideration that "tragedy depends to some extent upon individual responsibility, the realization of this responsibility and the inner growth evolving from this realization." What Mr. Nelson is saying is that people are responsible for their own doings provided their present situation has been truly motivated. Then, and only then, can a classic tragic character evolve. However, Nancy Tischner refutes the idea that Williams intended to write a classical tragedy: "He did not see Blanche as a Medea or an Electra. Her quality is pathetic softness, not tragic strength. Nor is there any catharsis to cleanse the audience of its distress when the action moves like a reversal of Darwin's vision-back to the apes. Our sense of justice and our love of beauty are outraged: we leave the theatre troubled, not tranquil."

Where does the strength of Williams' artistry lie? Technically, *A Streetcar Named Desire* is an almost flawless work. The plot of the play is advanced rapidly and excites a great deal of interest. Each scene is coordinated to the next and the slow revelation of all of the jigsaw parts of Blanche's character is adroitly done to create continuous anticipation for the audience. Williams' ability to develop strong and interesting characters is evident in Blanche and Stanley. Despite the discrepancies in social moral conduct, his psychological exposure of the ruthlessness of people is dramatically sound. His use of symbolism helps immeasurably to make them vivid; Blanche's horror of unshaded light bulbs expresses her inability to face reality, as Stanley's devotion to poker games and undershirts announces his virility. Stella is commonplace and finds complete gratification in marriage; the other characters are small, mean, frustrated, and violent. It is an exciting and colorful gallery. Williams finds it difficult to put words on paper without making them conform to a strong poetic nature. He writes dialogue that not only depicts subtleties of characterization but wastes little time in furthering the action of the story. Blanche's speech is lyrical and imaginary but there is no pause for poetizing. She is constantly expressing her maladjustment to a more modern idiom. Stanley is more in tune with reality by using a short, terse, inarticulate mode of speaking that also contains **imagism** but on a coarser level. The colloquial expressions of the other characters are also molded and shaped into a sense and rhythm that are unique and vital to the play.

Williams has a feeling for the use of comedy which is not unlike the bard William Shakespeare. Shakespeare used the Porter in *Macbeth* and the Grave Digger in *Hamlet* to allay tragic eventuality and to build a feeling of anticipation in the audience. In *Streetcar*, while Stanley is engaged in divulging all his condemning evidence about Blanche to Stella he is at the same time concerned about using the bathroom, which is occupied by Blanche. Unaware of the incriminating danger that awaits her as she emerges from the bathroom, Blanche answers Stanley's blows on the door with "possess your soul in patience" to which Stanley retorts, "It's not my soul, it's my kidneys I'm worried about." This is just one of the several moments of comedy used by Williams to enhance the effect of the seriousness of his drama.

The importance of *A Streetcar Named Desire* lies in its effect upon an audience. Brooks Atkinson, drama critic for the *New York Times* at the time of *Streetcar's* premiere on Broadway, had good opportunity to witness this effect and he concluded that "they come away from it profoundly moved. . . . Out of nothing more esoteric than interest in human beings, Mr. Williams has looked steadily and wholly into the private agony of one lost person."

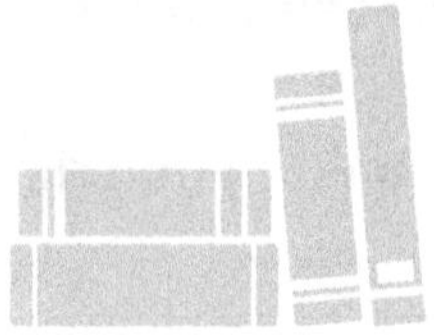

A STREETCAR NAMED DESIRE

ESSAY QUESTIONS AND ANSWERS

Question: Discuss the major symbols used in *A Streetcar Named Desire* and show how they are related to the drama.

Answer: The most obvious symbol used in the play is its title and the actual reference in the play to the streetcars named Desire and Cemeteries. They are the means by which Blanche was brought to the home of Stanley and Stella and as the play unfolds we realize the names of the streetcars have a greater significance. Blanche's instructions were "to take a streetcar named Desire, and then transfer to one called Cemeteries." When Blanche first arrives she is possessed by a desire for love and understanding, but always in the background lurks the fear of death and destruction. If the one cannot be obtained a transfer to the other will be the inevitable alternative. Blanche indicates this in her speech to Mitch in **scene nine**: "Death-I used to sit here and she used to sit over there and death was as close as you are. . . . We didn't dare even admit we had ever heard of it? The opposite is desire." A subtle use of the symbol makes **scene six** very poignant: Mitch and Blanche have just returned from the amusement park and Blanche, concerned about transportation to take Mitch home, is surprised to hear that Desire runs all night long. The two basic drives, desire and death, are persistent throughout the play in determining Blanche's total behavior.

The destination for Blanche's streetcar travels is Elysian Fields, which also has a symbolic significance to the play. It is the section of New Orleans in which Stanley and Stella live as well as a reference to Greek mythology meaning paradise. In *Streetcar*, Stanley and Stella have created their own type of paradise in the sensual and blissful existence in which they live. Ironically, the location has an opposite effect on Blanche. Instead of finding happiness and contentment she encounters nothing but sorrow and destruction. Perhaps one can go further in suggesting that Paradise was originally created for two. The intrusion of a third member caused sin and despair. Elysian Fields will never be the same for Stanley and Stella after Blanche's departure.

During Blanche's slow and inevitable journey toward insanity she is constantly looking for a means of escape. Realizing that satisfaction is impossible in the Kowalski household, she reaches out desperately to Mitch. When this means of escape becomes unattainable she creates an escape of her own, Shep Huntleigh. He is a symbol of the perfect gentleman for whom Blanche searched but never really found. She found him, however, in her world of fantasy. As Blanche's deterioration increases, Huntleigh becomes a more vital and dominant illusion for her.

In **scene nine** we hear the vendor's cry of the Mexican Woman, "Flores, flores para los muertos" (flowers, flowers for the dead). It follows the moment when Mitch denounces Blanche as a liar and thereupon refuses to marry her. The vendor's cry becomes symbolic of Blanche's failure to remain among the living. Blanche protests by shouting "No, no! Not now! Not now!" but the cry persists and in the following moment Blanche loses her hold on reality.

Constantly, throughout the play there is a continual reference to light. It is used in the form of bright sunlight, on the morning following Stella's beating at the hands of Stanley, indicating they have settled their grievances. It is used in the form of candlelight for the amorous isolation of Mitch and Blanche in **scene six**. But most important, it is used as a foil for Blanche. From the moment she viewed the death of her young husband, Blanche was aware that the bright searchlight of the world was extinguished and since that time, life to her has been nothing more than the flicker of a candle; and she intends to keep it that way for she is prepared to protect herself from the harsh light of reality with the use of a paper lantern. The paper lantern becomes a symbol of Blanche. She covers every bare light bulb for fear that her life of illusion will be discovered. Mitch finds the real Blanche by tearing the lantern from the light, and Stanley hands her the remains of her torn illusion in the very last moment of the play as she is being led away to an asylum.

Question: What is the main **theme** in *A Streetcar Named Desire*?

Answer: The play *A Streetcar Named Desire* is about Blanche DuBois; therefore, the main **theme** of the drama concerns her directly. In Blanche is seen the tragedy of an individual caught between two worlds-the world of the past and the world of the present-unwilling to let go of the past and unable, because of her character, to come to any sort of terms with the present. The final result is her destruction. This process began long before her clash with Stanley Kowalski. It started with the death of her young husband, a weak and perverted boy who committed suicide when she taunted him with her disgust at the discovery of his perversion. In retrospect, she knows that he was the only man she had ever loved, and from this early **catastrophe** evolves her promiscuity. She is lonely and frightened, and she attempts to fight this condition with sex. Desire fills the emptiness when there is no love and desire blocks the inexorable movement of death, which has already wasted and decayed Blanche's ancestral home Belle Reve.

For Blanche, Belle Reve was the remaining symbol of a life and tradition that she knows in her heart have vanished, yet to which she clings with a desperate tenacity. She is dated. Her speech, manners and habit are foolishly passed, but still she cannot abandon this sense of herself as someone special, as a "lady" in the grand tradition. She knows she is an **anachronism** in an alien world and yet she will not compromise. She cannot and will not surrender the dream she has of herself, and even though she wants desperately not to be lonely, it is precisely the clinging to this dream, the airs, mannerisms and sense of herself, which alienate her further. She is trapped in a terrifying contradiction. Her need to be special, to adhere to codes and a tradition no longer valid, creates an intense isolation, while simultaneously her desire not to be alone, to be loved, threatens to break through this isolation. It not only threatens, but does break through. Betrayed by love once in her life, she nevertheless seeks it in the effort to fill the lonely void; thus, her promiscuity. But to adhere to her tradition and her sense of herself as a lady, she cannot face this sensual part of herself. She associates it with the animalism of Stanley's love-making and terms it brutal desire. She feels guilt and a sense of sin when she does surrender to it, and yet she does, out of intense loneliness. By viewing sensuality as brutal desire she is able to disassociate it from what she feels is her true self, but only at the price of an intense inner conflict. Since she cannot integrate these conflicting elements of desire and gentility, she tries to reject the one-desire-and live solely by the other. Desperately seeking a haven she looks increasingly to fantasy. Taking refuge in tinsel, fine clothes, and rhinestones, and the illusion that a beau is available whenever she wants him, she seeks tenderness and beauty in a world of her own making.

Blanche is not really lost in illusions; rather she uses them as camouflage. She wears them as she wears her clothes and her glass necklaces, in protection from a reality which she finds horrifying. One must not think of Blanche as just a fragile, delicate blossom. There is a fierce desire in her for life at any cost. Her masquerade may be a defense against a brutal world, but it is a clawing, desperate defense. Tragically for Blanche, it is a losing defense. Blanche simply has too many strikes against her. Her past, the lies she must tell to conceal it, and her concept of herself as a Southern lady, all conspire to destroy her when Stanley Kowalski sets himself to the task of exposing her.

Question: Discuss the aspects of loneliness in the play.

Answer: Loneliness comes from an unfulfilled desire to be loved and needed. Blanche was lonely when she arrived at Elysian Fields, the home of Stanley and Stella Kowalski. She recognized this same condition in Mitch and thereby became attracted to him. Both are individuals who desperately attempt to achieve some kind of meaningful human communication and contact, but because of their respective characters and the situation in which they find themselves, are unable to succeed. Blanche's greatest dilemma is finding someone to take the place of the husband whom she loved and inadvertently lost. This search for love, for the need to fill the void within her, is the essential reason for her promiscuity. Mitch, too, is a victim of loneliness. Although bound to his aged mother, he is restless and unsatisfied. He feels incomplete and longs for someone who will give him a sense of wholeness. He, like Blanche, had loved once and lost. In the mutual need of Blanche and Mitch, and in their inability to fulfill this need, they beautifully and poignantly express the **theme** of loneliness.

Question: Compare the characters of Stella and Blanche.

Answer: The most obvious comparison between Stella and Blanche is that they are sisters, but this blood relationship suggests other similarities between the two women. They are both part of the final generation of a once aristocratic but now moribund family. Both manifest a great deal of culture and sensitivity, and because of this, both seem out of place in Elysian Fields. Blanche, of course, is much more of an **anachronism** than Stella, who has for the most part adapted to the environment of Stanley Kowalski. Finally, both Stella and Blanche are or have been married. It is in their respective marriages that we can begin to trace the profound differences between these two sisters.

Where Blanche's marriage proved catastrophic to her, Stella's marriage seems to be fulfilling her as a woman. Blanche's marriage to a young homosexual, and the subsequent tragedy that resulted from her discovery of her husband's degeneracy and her inability to help him, have been responsible for much of the perversity in her life; Stella's marriage to Stanley, on the other hand, seems to have given her the happiness and fulfillment which Blanche has attempted to fill in a guilt-ridden life of loneliness with promiscuity. As a result she has become neurotic and alcoholic, slipping increasingly into insanity. Stella, meanwhile, has been thriving in a profane, coarse, but wholly satisfying sexual relationship with Stanley. Thus, superficially, the main contrast between Stella and Blanche seems to be one between sickness and health, perversity and normality, particularly in the sexual relationship. Stella is thriving; Blanche is disintegrating. But a closer examination of these sisters begins to show more complex differences in their characters and situations. Blanche is disintegrating for reasons other than sexual perversity, and Stella is paying a rather steep price for her so-called "normal" life with Stanley.

Blanche is committed to a tradition and a way of life that have become anachronistic in the world of Stanley Kowalski. She is committed to a code of civilization that died with her ancestral home, Belle Reve. Stella recognizes this tradition and her sister's commitment to it, but she has chosen to relinquish it and to come to terms with a world that has no place for it. In a sense, Blanche is frantic in her refusal to relinquish her concept of herself as a lady belonging to a cultured and cultivated tradition, even though that tradition is all but dissipated. Stella, on the other hand, is the conformist, who has allowed herself to be pulled from the pillars of Belle Reve and has adapted to her new existence with the vital, amoral, and uncouth Stanley. But Stella has had to pay a high price for salvation: the submerging of every element in her character that makes her similar to Blanche-personal dignity, gentility, and the sense of herself as a lady. At the end of the play, Stella takes Eunice's advice and goes on living with Stanley even though she knows he has destroyed her sister. But this is not as much a triumph on Stella's part as it is a capitulation to the way things are. Blanche has been destroyed because of her commitment to some rather shopworn, but still noble ideals; Stella will thrive because she has paid a price Blanche could never pay: capitulation. Stella has chosen life, but life bereft of everything that, according to Blanche makes it meaningful. These choices, rather than their sexual relationships, are the main points of contrast between the sisters.

BIBLIOGRAPHY AND GUIDE TO FURTHER RESEARCH

Works by Tennessee Williams

American Blues: Five Short Plays. Dramatists Play Service, Inc., New York.

Baby Doll. New Directions. 1956.

Battle of Angels. New Directions.

Camino Real. New Directions.

Cat on a Hot Tin Roof. New Directions.

The Glass Menagerie. New Directions.

Hard Candy, A Book of Stories. New Directions.

I Rise in Flame, Cried the Phoenix. New Directions.

In the Winter of Cities. New Directions.

The Milk Train Doesn't Stop Here Anymore.

The Mutilated.

The Night of the Iguana.

One Arm and Other Stories. New Directions.

Orpheus Descending with Battle of Angels. New Directions.

Period of Adjustment. New Directions.

The Roman Spring of Mrs. Stone. New Directions.

The Rose Tattoo. New Directions.

A Streetcar Named Desire. New Directions.

Suddenly Last Summer. New Directions.

Summer and Smoke. New Directions.

Sweet Bird of Youth. New Directions.

Twenty-Seven Wagons Full of Cotton and Other One-Act Plays. New Directions.

Works about Tennessee Williams

Atkinson, Brooks "Theatre: Early Williams," *New York Times*, Nov. 22, 1956.

Barnett, Lincoln. "Tennessee Williams," *Life*, Feb. 16, 1948.

Bentley, Eric. *The Dramatic Event.* New York: Horizon Press, 1954.

____*In Search of Theatre.* New York: Alfred A. Knopf, 1953.

Carpenter, Charles A., Jr. and Elizabeth Cook. "Addenda to 'Tennessee Williams: A Selected Bibliography,'" *Modern Drama*, Dec. 1959.

Donahue, Francis. *The Dramatic World of Tennessee Williams*, New York, Frederick Ungar, 1964.

Dony, Nadine. "Tennessee Williams: A Selected Bibliography," *Modern Drama*, Dec. 1958.

Engle, Paul. "A Locomotive Named Reality," *The New Republic*, Jan. 24, 1955, pp. 26, 27.

Falk, Signi. *Tennessee Williams*. Grosset & Dunlap, Inc., 1961.

Ganz, Arthur. "The Desperate Morality of the Plays of Tennessee Williams," *American Scholar*, Spring 1962, pp. 278-294.

Gassner, John. "Tennessee Williams: Dramatist of Frustration," *College English*, Oct. 1948, pp. 1-7.

Goodman, Randolph. *Drama on Stage*. New York: Holt, Rinehart & Winston, 1961.

Jackson, Esther M. "The Broken World of Tennessee Williams," *Madison & Milwaukee*, University of Wisconsin Press, 1965.

Jones, Robert Emmet. "Tennessee Williams' Early Heroines," *Modern Drama*, Dec. 1959, pp. 211-219.

Krutch, Joseph Wood. *Modernism in Modern Drama*. Ithaca: Cornell University Press, 1953.

Lewis, R. C. "A Playwright Named Tennessee," *The New York Times Magazine*, Dec. 7, 1947, pp. 19, 67, 69-70.

Maxwell Gilbert. *Tennessee Williams and Friends*. New York: The World Pub. Co., 1965.

Moor, Paul. "A Mississippian Named Tennessee," *Harper's Magazine*, Jul. 1948, pp. 63-71.

Nelson, Benjamin. *Tennessee Williams: The Man and His Work*. New York, 1961. (The best of the full-length studies of Williams)

Popkin, Henry. "The Plays of Tennessee Williams," *Tulane Drama Review*, Spring 1960, pp. 45-64. (An excellent study of Williams' plays)

Sharp, William. "An Unfashionable View of Tennessee Williams," *Tulane Drama Review*, Mar. 1962, pp. 160-171.

Taylor, Harry. "The Dilemma of Tennessee Williams," *Masses and Mainstream*, Apr. 1948, pp. 51-56.

Tischler, Nancy M. *Tennessee Williams: Rebellious Puritan*. New York: Citadel Press, 1961. (Interesting study of plays in the context of William's biography.)

Tynan, Kenneth. "American Blues, The Plays of Arthur Miller and Tennessee Williams," *Encounter*, May 1954, pp. 13-19.

____"Valentine to Tennessee Williams," *Mademoiselle*, Feb. 1956.

Vowles, Richard B. "Tennessee Williams: The World of His Imagery," *Tulane Drama Review*, Dec. 1958, pp. 51-56.

Williams, Tennessee. "Tennessee Williams on the Past, the Present and the Perhaps," *New York Times*, Mar. 17, 1957.

www.ingramcontent.com/pod-product-compliance
Lightning Source LLC
Chambersburg PA
CBHW061517050726
47593CB00002B/605

* 9 7 8 1 6 4 5 4 2 4 1 6 1 *